WHAT IS THIS BITCOIN THING?

Should you be making money
with cryptocurrency?
Get up to speed with this beginner's guide
to the bitcoin opportunity

MARCO HØDD

For permission requests, speaking inquiries, and bulk order purchase options, please email:
info@marcohodd.com

First Edition: October 2022

Paperback ISBN: 978-1-7391963-0-1

Hardback ISBN: 978-1-7391963-1-8

ABOUT THE AUTHOR.
AND A STRANGE MAN IN THE BAR.

A few years ago, I moved out of the corporate 9 to 5 world. I was bored, and I wanted to do something a bit more entrepreneurial. I was creating my own products to sell on Amazon. It was different from anything I'd done before. Part of the excitement was going to China to meet with manufacturers to select products for my new outdoor lifestyle brand.

I met many amazing people who were all building their own businesses in a similar way. I really enjoyed talking to people from all walks of life in the bar at the end of the day. One person that I met early in 2017 struck me in particular. He was quite 'strange.' Strange in the sense that he wasn't focusing much of his energy on the whole purpose of the trip—to find new suppliers and products. He wasn't especially curious about anyone else's business. He was more interested in telling people about things HE found interesting, which didn't seem at all related to finding new products in China. He joined a group of us after dinner for a couple of hours but didn't appear to be listening to much of the conversation. As others drifted off to bed, I was left sitting with this chap, and he started to talk to me. He said, "You know what... you're making money on Amazon, yes?" Yes, I said. "Well, don't reinvest it all back in the business. If you're making a profit, put it into bitcoin."

It was the start of a long conversation. His eyes lit up, he got very excited about the subject, and he was trying to communicate why it was important. I was interested in what he was saying, but at the same time, I found a lot of what he was talking about to be quite impenetrable. There was a lot of technical jargon. I wondered whether this bitcoin thing was accessible to a 'normal' person.

He said, "When you get home... my recommendation to you is, whatever you do, go and buy $100 worth of bitcoin. And then you'll begin to find out about it."

I found the whole conversation intriguing. I thought quite a lot about this bitcoin thing over the following days. When I got home, with the first spare time I had, I sat in front of my computer and started digging around on the subject. And to be honest, I found the whole thing quite difficult. I persevered. I found some helpful blogs and guides online, and eventually, I figured out how to buy some bitcoin and store it.

I'd done it! I had $100 worth of bitcoin. But it wasn't easy to do, to be honest. Banks didn't like you moving money to foreign banks to buy bitcoin, and credit card companies were banning bitcoin purchases.

But that act of buying some bitcoin for the first time, 'switched' me on. I started noticing articles and news related to bitcoin and slowly started learning. Now that I've learned a whole lot more, I've realized that there is so much garbage and dross out there that people talk about in relation to the entire field of crypto technology. And this muddles all the excellent information and advice that is out there.

There is a massive opportunity for people to participate in this new technology. Still, sadly the majority of people haven't got a clue about it or a clue how to start participating. I can see the potential risk that this vast area of technology takes off, leaving a mass of people behind.

I'm less interested in the nuts and bolts of technology—how the underlying blockchain technology works—and I'm more interested in what this new technology can do for us as human beings. How will this technology affect our countries, economies, societies, families, work, and relationships? All of these are going to be impacted to a greater or lesser extent through the advent of crypto applications of all sorts, many of which are currently unimaginable.

TABLE OF CONTENTS

YOUR FREE GIFT

I'd like to say thank you for buying *"What is this crypto thing?"* So I've put together a survival guide that will be an essential companion as you start your exploration of the crypto world.

The *Crypto Survival Quick Start Guide* will keep you safe. It's an action summary and checklist that will show you:

- How to DYOR—"Do Your Own Research"
- Dangers of crypto to avoid—and how to stay SAFE
- Specific NEXT STEPS to further your learning

I've created the guide to be fun, fast to consume, and action-oriented. It's precisely what I wish I'd had five years ago when I first dipped my toes into crypto waters.

Get your Crypto Survival Quick Start Guide here:
https://marcohodd.com/crypto-survival

INTRODUCTION

Most of us have heard about bitcoin and cryptocurrency—even if we don't know what these terms mean. Despite the amount of news coverage this new technology receives, relatively few individuals are actively participating in the crypto opportunity.

There will no doubt be many reasons for this...
I'm not tech-savvy.
It doesn't interest me.
I think it's risky.
I wouldn't know where to start.
It's too confusing.
I've missed the boat.
It's not something I need.

I've shared my enthusiasm for crypto with many, many people. Occasionally I meet a fellow enthusiast, and we greedily trade our knowledge and experience. But for the most part, whenever I talk to someone about bitcoin or cryptocurrency, they feign interest for about 30 seconds, and then I see their eyes glaze over. I know I have to stop because I'm losing them.

Helping people to REALLY understand about bitcoin and cryptocurrency has become a major obsession of mine. No one needs to be a rocket scientist to understand and feel confident about this new technology. No one needs to be left behind as this exciting new technology takes off and brings a whole host of new opportunities.

Getting started is sometimes very hard. You don't know what to pay attention to and what not. So this book is unashamedly a 'beginner's guide.' It will focus on bitcoin—the biggest cryptocurrency—and for the most part, ignore other cryptocurrencies. It will present a clear and simple explanation of bitcoin technology. No excessive jargon—just what you need to REALLY understand what this bitcoin thing is, and (just enough about) how it works.

I've brought everything together in one place so you can decide whether it makes sense for you to invest or not. And I provide an easy-to-follow process for buying and storing some bitcoin.

My name is Marco Hødd, and I've spent my entire career helping people to understand and benefit from new technologies and systems. I'm not a technologist—I'm a people person. I know how to translate techno-speak into everyday language so everyone can understand and participate, should they choose to.

At the beginning of my working life, the Internet arrived. I fumbled with the early technology and followed its journey to the most incredible life-changing resource we all use today. Like the Internet back then, cryptocurrency is just beginning its journey. And like many others, I am fumbling with it, and looking forward to the ride.

Crypto isn't just about money—the technology enables a whole host of new possibilities. Once you understand a little about bitcoin, and perhaps you have bought a small amount, you'll start to pay attention to all the bright shiny innovations that are taking place. I'll get you ready for your next steps with a taster of some of these towards the end of this book.

Helping friends and family take their first steps in the world of crypto is something I've been actively doing for almost two years. I've got good at reducing things down to the essentials. I've created 'mini guides' for people. I've created a short 'how to' video series. And all the while, I'm reading, researching, and playing to stay up-to-date.

That's right. PLAYING. I promise that if you play in the crypto sand pit, you will learn. Active participation opens you up to learning in a way that's just not possible by looking on from the sidelines. Investing just a tiny amount makes you a participant. This book will help you make your own decision about whether to take this first step.

"The best time to plant a tree was twenty years ago. The second best time is now."

I bet you've heard that one before. I think the same is very true about participating in bitcoin. But as you will learn in Chapter 1—it is still very early. So tomorrow, or the day after, is fine too.

What you are about to learn in this book will open up a whole new world to you. As you work through each short chapter, you'll build your understanding of bitcoin. You'll be able to decide whether you want to participate, and you'll have all the support you need to make your very first investment in bitcoin. You'll no longer be a 'no coiner.' You'll be a PLAYER!

1. BEGINNING.
AND WE ARE STILL BEGINNING.

Who developed bitcoin?

On Halloween in 2008, a computer scientist named Satoshi Nakamoto published a whitepaper that described a new digital currency. The paper was called "Bitcoin: A Peer-to-Peer Electronic Cash System." (1) It promised a new way for people to send and receive money without going through any sort of bank or financial institution. The world had been introduced to blockchains and cryptocurrencies. And on January 3, 2009, Nakamoto launched bitcoin as the first ever cryptocurrency when he created the first-ever 'block' on the first-ever blockchain.

But incredibly, no one knows who Satoshi Nakamoto is! His self-created profile lists him as a 45-year-old male from Japan. But many people doubt that. Despite years of speculation, nothing more has been confirmed about Nakamoto's real identity.

On April 26, 2011, Nakamoto sent a final email to fellow bitcoin developers stating that he had "moved on to other projects." He has not been heard from since. It's estimated that Nakamoto holds around 1 million bitcoins, valued currently at about $21 billion—all of which to this day remain untouched.

This astonishing beginning has led to a roller coaster ride for the new cryptocurrency, bitcoin. Thirteen years later, interest in bitcoin and thousands of other cryptocurrencies has never been stronger. Crypto is here to stay.

Why is bitcoin's price so volatile?

We'll look at some factors that drive bitcoin's price a little later. But in a nutshell, bitcoin's price volatility is unsurprising. This technology is new, and it is developing at a furious pace. Huge amounts of entrepreneurial activity is powering this technology forwards as we've never seen before. And the vast majority of people have low levels of awareness and understanding about what's happening.

Think back to the early days of the Internet. The landscape was very similar indeed. I was in my mid-20s when I first downloaded the software I needed to send and receive email and browse the world wide web. It was complex and clunky.

If you were not technically inclined, you weren't participating then. It was several years before the technology matured sufficiently for some early tech companies to start luring the masses to set up a CompuServe email account, download the Mosaic browser and try out the World Wide Web.

Things started going crazy. Remember? Thousands of 'Internet' companies were popping up in all sectors. All were propelling the technology forwards at a blistering pace. Few of them made any money—but that didn't matter then. It was all about technology and growth. And then the prize at the end of the line was an 'IPO'—going public via a share offer which went stratospheric because the company's name ended with 'dot-com.' Companies like Amazon, eBay, Priceline, and LastMinute.com were created. But this pace was unsustainable.

On March 10, 2020, the Nasdaq composite index hit an all-time high of 5132.50, and investor sentiment turned from buy buy buy to sell sell sell. This signaled the start of the dot-com bubble burst. The index lost half its value within a year and hit bottom on October 10, 2002, at 1108.40. It would be almost 15 years until the Nasdaq Composite crossed 5000 again!

The bubble popped, and there was a big shakeout. More than 80% of these startups vanished from sight. I remember Pets.com, Gov.works, Broadcast.com, Geocities, Boo.com, and eXite. So many amazing ideas and fledgling businesses failed to make it, but they all contributed to the collective development and maturity of the new Internet world.

A number of notable tech companies survived. They climbed back after the crash and thrived—Amazon, eBay, Priceline, tech companies Adobe, Intuit, IBM, Oracle, SanDisk, and chip-related companies ARM, and ASML. But they had to endure a devastating correction to their share prices. Amazon's share price crashed 90% during this period and didn't achieve an all-time high again until the early 2010s.

A bubble is a natural endpoint to a period of growth and innovation. A shakeout. Winners and losers.

Right now, crypto is in its early stages, just like the Internet was back then. There is incredible growth and development as tech entrepreneurs fuse technology with their imaginations to bring all sorts of innovations to our attention. Some will undoubtedly have significant long-term impacts on how we lead our lives. Others will be total duds.

The price of bitcoin over the past thirteen years is a picture of volatility. Ever-changing supply and demand that reacts dramatically to news about the technology, economy, environment, and political landscape. But as bitcoin grows and regulatory support develops, the cryptocurrency becomes a little more stable—although it's still the wild west compared to 'traditional' financial products and markets.

As I write (June 2022), the entire crypto market is experiencing one of the worst crashes in its short history. There's nothing fundamentally wrong with crypto technologies and projects, but they are being impacted to a considerable degree by the broader macroeconomy. This month, a World Bank press release cites COVID-19 and the Russian invasion of Ukraine as magnifying the global economic slowdown, and the beginning of a protracted period of little growth and high inflation. (2) Many of us are experiencing the harsh effects of persistent disturbances in the supply chains of goods and services, substantial price increases for energy consumers, and punishing fiscal policies that attempt to keep inflation under control.

Crypto is not immune to this broader economic context. Since bitcoin reached its all-time high of over $68,000 in November 2021, the market has been falling to the current price of around $20,000. That's 70% below the all-time high. Other cryptocurrencies have suffered the same fate—many shedding 80-90% of their value. If you've heard anything about the collapse of TerraUSD, you'll know that some cryptos have suffered even more.

For now, anyway, volatility comes with the territory. A more stable crypto economy will emerge as mainstream adoption begins. Just like it did for the Internet economy.

Will I understand this?

The technology we are starting to see is far too varied and complex to feature comprehensively in any 'introductory' book. That's why I have chosen to focus solely on bitcoin. Once the reader has a good understanding of bitcoin, it's so much easier to broaden that understanding to other technologies in the crypto space.

I am unapologetic about leaving out the other many crypto topics in this book—it's all too easy to disappear down a rabbit hole! I don't want any reader to feel overwhelmed, out of their depth, or confused. Frankly, and thankfully, you don't need to know everything about cryptography, economic theory, financial wizardry, and blockchain technology to understand bitcoin.

I want every reader to develop their understanding gradually and confidently. I have banished techno-babble and complexity from this book wherever possible. I have done my best to be accurate—but I have had to simplify things, and I will have made a few mistakes along the way. This is inevitable with such a complex and ever-changing landscape.

My starting position is that I believe crypto to be one of the most transformational technologies developing today. And also the least understood. The 'average person,' if there was such a person, doesn't have much of a clue. I want to try and explain how this technology works in plain non-tech speak and what potential it has for us all.

If you read further books on the subject, you may notice the bias of authors. Some are evangelical about bitcoin and how it will solve all of the world's economic problems. Others take a less enthusiastic stance aiming for a 'realistic' appraisal of the technology. Personally, I am a massive enthusiast about all things crypto. But I'm not here to convert you—I'm here simply to answer the question, "What is this bitcoin thing?" And I'm going to suggest a way that you can dip your toe in the water.

Before writing this book, I looked into the most common bitcoin-related questions that were being asked on the

Internet. The majority of questions could be summarized under three headings:

- What is bitcoin, and how does it work?
- How is bitcoin's price determined, and why is it so volatile?
- How do I buy bitcoin, and where is it stored?

This book will certainly answer those questions for you. But it will also answer other critical questions that perhaps you haven't asked yet. Questions that will help you REALLY understand what this bitcoin thing is.

Am I too late?

I am sure you will answer this question for yourself as you read on. But in a word, no. You are early. As you shall see, bitcoin is still very much in its infancy.

Don't pay any attention to bitcoin's price. Instead, focus on the potential of the technology and ask yourself whether the demand for bitcoin in the future will be greater than the demand for bitcoin today.

Of course, no one really knows where this new technology will take us—in the same way that we couldn't envisage the pervasiveness of the Internet back in the early 1990s. But I hope this book gives you a bird's eye view—enough to see that regardless of where the technology goes, its future is exciting and bright. And it probably looks nothing like it does today!

By the end of this book, I hope that all readers can make an informed choice about whether to participate, or whether to spectate at this stage of bitcoin's development.

1.

"Bitcoin: A Peer-to-Peer Electronic Cash System"

Bitcoin.org

https://bitcoin.org/en/bitcoin-paper

2.

"Stagflation Risk Rises Amid Sharp Slowdown in Growth"

The World Bank, June 7, 2022

https://www.worldbank.org/en/news/press-release/2022/06/07/stagflation-risk-rises-amid-sharp-slowdown-in-growth-energy-markets

2. A STORY ABOUT EL SALVADOR

When I started writing this chapter, the news was full of stories about Venezuela being on a path to adopt bitcoin as a legal currency. Hyperinflation was causing economic chaos and wiping out people's savings. But then El Salvador stole the 'limelight' to become the first country to make bitcoin legal tender on September 7, 2021.

Many other countries have suffered the devastating effects of hyperinflation. More often than not, the causes aren't homegrown and have resulted from complex trade and political relationships with other economies. Well-intentioned monetary control doesn't keep pace with economic hardships. New money is printed. And then more is printed. Before long, there is so much more new money in circulation that the currency's value starts to drop. Over time, this can lead to extreme situations where a currency becomes practically useless.

Imagine being given $1 in the morning that is only worth 1¢ by the end of the day! People are forced to adopt a barter system because money has become worthless. In recent history, Brazil, North Korea, Peru, Yugoslavia, and Zimbabwe have all suffered from periods of crippling hyperinflation. But I'll use the example of El Salvador to explain why bitcoin provides a new way to stabilize an economy that's rocketed out of control.

What was El Salvador's economic problem?

El Salvador experienced a long period of civil war from the late 1970s through to the early 1990s. The unrest was accompanied by rising inflation—sometimes exceeding 20% per annum. Following the war, the government decided to 'peg' its currency against the dollar to reduce inflation, and by the late 1990s, the economy had returned to general stability. The government went further in 2001 by adopting the US dollar as its official currency to bring in more investment and spur economic growth.

With 'dollarization,' the government promised the arrival of abundant investments, more exports, and quality jobs. None of which ever actually arrived. Imports continued to exceed exports, with average annual economic growth contracting and public debt exceeding GDP in 2021.

Dollarization did provide some benefits. For instance, El Salvador has not faced hyperinflation like some of its Latin American counterparts have.

However, under the dollarization regime, El Salvador had no control over its own monetary policy. By adopting the US dollar as its official currency, El Salvador had ceded its authority over money supply and interest rates to the Federal Reserve. It is doubtful that the Fed will consider the needs of a country the size of El Salvador when determining interest rates. Therefore, the Salvadoran government had to depend on taxes and spending to stimulate the economy since it no longer had control over money supply and interest rates. This caused El Salvador to run higher deficits through the last decade. The government had to raise expenditures to stimulate the economy instead of decreasing interest rates to spur consumption and investment.

What did they decide to do?

The majority of the population regarded the impacts of dollarization as largely damaging to El Salvador's economy. (1) But with opposing views on the political left and political right, sufficient support for de-dollarization has been hard to achieve in government. The country's current president,

Nayib Bukele, is a centralist whose views on de-dollarization align with the traditional right.

Bukele proposed introducing bitcoin as legal tender in El Salvador—a first-mover strategy to unlock lagging growth. (2) This is seen by many as a radical 'experiment.' But clearly, existing economic models have not served many Central and South American countries well, and adopting bitcoin brings new possibilities for economic stability and prosperity.

I shall explain precisely why countries like El Salvador look at bitcoin as a better system of money a little later in the book after we've covered some of the foundational principles of bitcoin.

What's happening now?

On September 7, 2021, El Salvador's Bitcoin Law came into effect, and bitcoin was legal tender for the very first time. Taxes may be paid in cryptocurrency, and merchants must accept it alongside the US dollar, the national currency since 2001. (3)

Just over a month later, more Salvadorans have bitcoin wallets than traditional bank accounts. According to government figures, three million people have downloaded the government's new Chivo (which means 'cool' in local slang) digital wallet, amounting to 46% of the population— whereas only around a third of Salvadorans have bank accounts.

The widespread adoption of the Chivo wallet is impressive, especially in comparison to traditional banking. But El Salvador is a country where few of the poorest citizens have access to bank accounts, but they do have the essential technology to adopt bitcoin—smartphones. The company Strike is behind the development of the Chivo wallet to enable payments to be made instantly for free via the Bitcoin Lightning Network.

Crypto enthusiasts are excited by the boldness of this move by El Salvador's president, but locals are less enthusiastic. Opinion polls show that a majority are against adopting bitcoin as a currency. This may be because there is a poor understanding of bitcoin and may also reflect little international support for bitcoin adoption.

The International Monetary Fund has warned against adopting cryptocurrencies as legal tender, citing risks to macroeconomic stability, financial integrity, consumer protection, and the environment. The World Bank has refused to advise El Salvador on bitcoin, and Moody's has downgraded the country's debt further into junk territory. (4) And spending a little time with Google reveals that the press is showing little support for El Salvador's experiment and Nayib Bukele's motives.

I'm no economist, but it seems obvious to me that the economic challenges faced by many countries in the region—lagging growth and high inflation—aren't going to be fixed by a few tweaks here and there. Something radical is called for to bring economies under control.

El Salvador and bitcoin is a process of innovation in action. There are supporters, and there are many opponents. As with all new technology adoptions, the journey will be bumpy, and no one can be certain of the outcomes. Except for one—the world will learn an enormous amount from El Salvador's pioneering actions.

Stories like El Salvador's are fast changing. While writing this book, the Central African Republic became the second country to adopt bitcoin as legal tender. (5) The mineral-rich country is one of the world's poorest, with almost three-quarters of the population living below the international poverty line. It has been experiencing violence and political instability for years. The adoption of bitcoin is seen as an opportunity to attract new investors to the country and create economic growth. Despite an ambitious vision, the

Central African Republic lags far behind El Salvador in terms of its infrastructure—over 80% of Central Africans do not have access to the Internet.

By the time you read this, the landscape will have changed further. Perhaps other countries will have adopted bitcoin as legal tender. Maybe there will be a runaway success story. Or adoption difficulties. Or a disaster. Countries suffering from the effects of hyperinflation will most likely be jumping into crypto experiments too.

Where people are suffering in crippled economies—they 'get' bitcoin. It is a no-brainer. It stops their money from losing its spending power. And a mobile phone is the only requirement to participate.

1.
"The Socioeconomic Implications of Dollarization in El Salvador"
Marcia Towers and Silvia Borzutzky, Latin American Politics and Society, 2004
https://www.jstor.org/stable/4141619

2.
"An Economic History Of El Salvador's Adoption Of Bitcoin"
Forbes, June 27, 2021
https://www.forbes.com/sites/rogerhuang/2021/06/27/an-economic-history-of-el-salvadors-adoption-of-bitcoin

3.

"In El Salvador, More People Have Bitcoin Wallets Than Traditional Bank Accounts"

Forbes, October 7, 2021

https://www.forbes.com/sites/theapothecary/2021/10/07/in-el-salvador-more-people-have-bitcoin-wallets-than-traditional-bank-accounts

4.

"El Salvador's dangerous gamble on bitcoin"

Financial Times, September 7, 2021

https://www.ft.com/content/c257a925-c864-4495-9149-d8956d786310

5.

"Central African Republic becomes second country to adopt bitcoin as legal tender"

CNBC, April 28, 2022

https://www.cnbc.com/2022/04/28/central-african-republic-adopts-bitcoin-as-legal-tender.html

3. NOW GIVE ME MONEY, (THAT'S WHAT I WANT)

What happened before we had money?

The first major Motown hit record told us that "lovin' don't pay my bills." But we haven't always had money. Ancient human tribes bartered—the first form of economic exchange. I want some bread, and I have some fish to offer you in exchange. I could also owe you the fish at some point in the future if you trust me. But often, I won't have something you want, or you don't know me well enough to trust me. So barter as a system of exchange has its limits.

The creation of money solves these problems with the barter system. It brings four main benefits.

Firstly, as a medium of exchange—a way of making payments. To be a good medium of exchange, the money needs to be widely accepted wherever it is being used.

Secondly, as a store of value—a way of ensuring that the money will be worth the same in the future as it is today. A good store of value ensures that money will buy you about the same amount of goods and services in the future.

Thirdly, as a way of transporting value—a way of easily moving the money to where it is needed. Money that is small and light is much easier to use than if it is large and heavy.

And fourthly, as a means of comparing the value of items. This requires that the money is widely accepted and has a stable price.

But even today, the currencies we use daily (referred to as 'fiat' currencies) don't perform equally well in all four respects just described. For example, the US dollar is a very effective medium of exchange in many parts of the world, it's easily transported electronically, and it's an excellent way to compare the value of different items—but it's a poor store of value over time. $1 in 1913 has the same purchasing power as $26 in 2020. (1)

How does a currency work?

To solve the problems of barter and the difficulties of transporting our wealth, we needed to find some 'currency' that everyone valued and was happy to exchange their goods and services for. The first examples of such a currency were scarce, precious metals like gold. Small pieces or coins of gold were easy to transport and could be used to buy goods and services.

To be good money, our currency needs certain properties— durable, light, uniform, fungible (one unit is identical to another), and relatively scarce. If everyone agrees that a coin made of gold has value, then it makes for good money.

Although the Chinese were first to create coins in around 770 BC, it was 100 years later that a region in Turkey began to mint coins from a naturally occurring mixture of gold and silver called electrum. The coins were of different sizes with different designs for different values. On the back of this innovation, Turkey's Ottoman empire grew to become the world's most dominant power for a while.

To this day, gold is a strong form of money. It's difficult and expensive to mine—so it's hard to increase the supply of gold very much, and the price of gold does not suffer much inflation. Although gold is no longer a practical 'medium of exchange' in our modern world, gold is still used widely as a store of value.

After the introduction of coins, it was another 1500 years until the next significant money innovation, which solved the difficulties and risks of transporting larger amounts of gold coins. The Chinese Tang dynasty invented the first ever paper money in around 800 AD. The paper notes issued could be redeemed for gold in China's capital anytime. Having a gold reserve that backed the paper currency created the trust required for everyone to use the notes as a form of money. Adoption was also ensured as the currency was controlled by the government, which outlawed all other forms of currency! (2)

Surprisingly, it took a further 500 years for the Europeans to catch on to the idea of paper money, when the first banknotes were issued in Sweden in 1661. Since then, paper has reigned supreme. Only in relatively recent years are we starting to see a decline in the use of paper money as electronic systems become more prevalent.

What's the problem with paper money?

Money has been around for our whole lifetime. We accept it, and we're used to it. We almost don't recognize some of the in-built problems of our system of money, and we have to remind ourselves about what doesn't work too well.

Confucian scholars made the most amazingly accurate prediction when the Chinese introduced paper money. They warned that the paper money would lead to government printing and weakening their currency. They argued that money should be left in the hands of the private market, which would make sure it stayed competitive and held value.

Four hundred years passed, and the new system of paper money worked well. You could go to the capital and swap your paper notes for an equivalent amount of gold or silver. But then the Chin dynasty got greedy and stopped backing the paper money with the gold and silver reserves. This was the first example of legal tender not backed by any asset.

They started printing money out of thin air, and China experienced the first-ever example of hyperinflation, where the value of paper money fell, and prices rose. In a period of just 50 years, the currency depreciated by almost 100%. By 1455 merchants were refusing paper money because it was worthless. The prediction of those Confucian scholars turned out to be rather perceptive! Paper money was eliminated, and the country returned to a silver-based economy until the 20th century.

Similarly, with the introduction of banknotes in Sweden 200 years later (3), some officials and merchants predicted that paper money would herald the downfall of the country's monetary system. But backed by the government's guarantee, banknotes were an immediate success as an alternative to carrying large, heavy, easily stolen quantities of gold or silver.

Other European governments observed Sweden's experiment and saw the convenience and safety of the banknotes and the boost that the economy experienced. It didn't take long for other European countries to start issuing their own paper money.

By the 19th century, most of the major countries understood that paper money had to be backed by hard assets to prevent it from becoming worthless over time. About 50 countries adopted the 'gold standard,' with the British pound being the dominant global currency at the time. Every note of paper money issued was backed by an equal amount of gold held in a country's reserves. This widespread system of money enabled a massive economic leap to happen during this period—what we know as the 'Industrial Revolution' today.

In common with the monetary failure experienced during the Chin dynasty, currencies that have departed from the gold standard have experienced problems. World War I caused Germany to break the link with gold in order to pay for military action—and many other countries dropped the gold standard for the same reason. When Germany lost the war, they were economically destroyed. In addition to repaying debt, they had to pay significant financial reparations. The currency hyper-inflated and failed, resulting in extreme economic hardship for the majority of the German people.

The two world wars in Europe enabled the United States to act as the bank. They sold weapons and supplies. They loaned money to Britain and France. Most of it was paid for in gold—and by the end of the war, America possessed around two-thirds of the world's gold reserves. On the back of this power, the US dollar became the world's new global reserve currency, backed by gold. And in this post-war world, most major global currencies were 'pegged' to the US dollar and a period of economic stability and enormous growth and prosperity ensued.

But, as we know, history repeats itself, and another war wreaked havoc on the global economy. During the Vietnam war, the United States started borrowing large amounts of money and then started printing the money it needed. Countries worldwide lost confidence that there was sufficient gold to back the dollar fully, and so started changing their dollars back and pulling their gold out of the United States. This was precisely the mistake made in Europe earlier in the century.

President Nixon had no option but to pull the dollar off the gold standard in 1971, and inevitably, massive devaluation of the dollar followed. The US dollar became what we call a 'fiat' currency. One declared by the government to be legal tender but not backed by any asset. The fact is that the US dollar has no intrinsic value whatsoever. The value of the US dollar is solely determined by everyone's agreement about the currency's utility.

So although our fiat currencies provide a store of value, they are not good stores of value. We know that the buying power of our currencies reduces over time. In ten years, my $100, £100, or ₹1000 will not be able to buy what it does today.

Governments have become used to balancing the books by printing more money. Unlike gold, money is very easy to 'mine.' But printing money is a short-term fix and essentially kicks the can down the road for the next set of politicians and policymakers to deal with. Printing money inflates the economy so that each unit of the currency is worth less.

The COVID pandemic provides us with the best recent example. Fighting the COVID-induced recession has caused the US government to print unprecedented amounts of money to stimulate the economy. The growth rate of all the dollars in circulation soared to a historic record of 27% in 2020-2021! To put this in some perspective, this compares with a figure of 10% during the financial crisis of 2007-2008. (4)

I hope you can see why gold is a good store of value now. Should we all move back to gold? Well, perhaps. But as we've already stated, gold has some of its own problems that need to be overcome.

The full story of money is not for this book—I just wanted to demonstrate a repeating pattern in our money system and the consequences of moving away from a 'hard' currency, or a currency 'backed' by a 'hard' asset like gold.

What state are we in now?

Today most major economies are spending more money than they are making. Everyone knows that if that continues, you will go bankrupt.

Governments are fuelling their economies by pumping them full of money and getting the economy into more and more trouble. Levels of debt in the United States reached 137% of the Gross Domestic Product in 2021—$28.43 trillion. Japan and China are the biggest holders of US debt, holding $1.30 trillion and $1.06 trillion, respectively. (5)

Again, this is not the subject of this book. But you don't need to read much else to know that many economies are on a knife edge because of their debt levels—just a whisker away from defaulting, or a massive currency devaluation.

Our governments have an abysmal record of managing our money. To avoid defaulting on our financial obligations, we must raise taxes and cut spending. As I write this chapter, the United States is maintaining its hardline policy to raise interest rates in an effort to reduce inflation. But such policies are unpopular with voters, and it is perhaps just a question of time before the money printer gets switched on again in time for the next election. Printing money certainly makes the debt seem smaller—but it takes the economy closure to wipe-out.

Every major economy engages in this political game—purposely devaluing the currency to stay competitive. The game is to walk a tightrope between lowering the currency to remain competitive without triggering hyperinflation and economic disaster.

We abandoned the backing of gold and are printing money at record levels. We know how this ends. Badly. Historically, we have always returned to 'hard money.' But this time, we have an alternative to gold—one that is harder and more secure. Bitcoin.

Perhaps the lyric of that 1959 Motown hit should be re-written, "Now give me (hard) money, (That's what I want)."

1.

"Purchasing Power of the US Dollar Over Time"

Visual Capitalist, April 6, 2021

https://www.visualcapitalist.com/purchasing-power-of-the-u-s-dollar-over-time

2.

"Keep your hands off my stack..."

Ep.3 The Crypto Exposé Podcast, November 30, 2019

https://anchor.fm/thecryptoexpose/episodes/Keep-your-hands-off-my-stack-e98ved

3.

"A History of Printed Money"

The International Bank Note Society

https://www.theibns.org/joomla/index.php?option=com_content&view=article&id=251

4.

"Understanding the Money Supply Increase in the US and its Potential Consequences"

Wheaton College, 2021

https://www.wheaton.edu/academics/academic-centers/wheaton-center-for-faith-politics-and-economics/resource-center/articles/2021/understanding-the-money-supply

5.

"United States Gross Federal Debt to GDP"

Trading Economics

https://tradingeconomics.com/united-states/government-debt-to-gdp

4. YOUR MONEY ISN'T YOUR MONEY

What is the case for bitcoin?

Money has always had to solve two big problems—to enable trading to take place between parties and to store value to allow it to be moved around easily. You either have to own currency in the form of physical items like banknotes and coins—or have a trusted institution like a bank track how much money you have.

Today, physical money is still difficult to move around. Large amounts are bulky and heavy, and of course, there are all sorts of legal restrictions about moving cash around— safeguards against unscrupulous activities. And you need to keep it secure so that it isn't stolen.

Even cash within the banking system is hard to move around. There are a multitude of checks and balances— inquisitions about where the money has come from, proof that the funds are yours, and proof that you are who you say you are. Sending money across international borders also requires currency conversion.

Trusted institutions like banks remove the difficulties of managing physical money, offer an accurate record of your money, and enable you to make speedy, secure, digital payments. These intermediaries are very much a feature of today's money system. We have banks, brokers, exchange merchants—all sorts of people who look after, move, exchange, and insure our money as it moves around the financial networks. These people sit between the end recipients of our financial transactions and us. And they all take a cut, which makes things more expensive and slower. And because of the complexity of steps and the parties involved, transactions can fail—they are not foolproof.

We are also all too aware of the risks of fraud in our current money system. Current levels of security are ever-improving, but there are always scammers who cleverly exploit weaknesses to gain control of our assets. We give over control of our personal data to these trusted third parties, and there are many examples of account hacking where personal data has been stolen. In 2014, JP Morgan Chase revealed that a massive computer hack had affected the accounts of 76m households. The hackers accessed names, telephone numbers, emails, and physical address information. (1) In 2017, Equifax reported that hackers could access the names, social security numbers, dates of birth, credit card numbers, and driver's license numbers of over 147m consumers. (2) In 2019, Capital One announced that data from around 100m people had been illegally accessed. (3)

Then there's the issue of privacy—another problem with money. We are being watched. There are triggers now on relatively small financial transactions that mean your details are being reported. Understandably we watch out for financial transactions that may involve crime, drugs, terrorism etc. But as a consequence, you and I, who are carrying out perfectly legal transactions, are being watched. We can debate whether that is a good thing or not. But the fact is that the current system does not facilitate any level of privacy.

And on top of all of this, the money in your bank account isn't actually YOUR money.

There is no vault that keeps your money safe. Once you deposit money, banks loan it to other banks, and those banks do the same. Currently, the Federal Reserve requires that a bank keep a minimum of 10% of its money in reserves—but the rest can be loaned. Other major countries have similar requirements. If we all went to the bank and demanded our money be paid back, they couldn't give it to us.

We call it a 'bank run' when large groups of customers of a bank or other financial institution all attempt to pull out their money simultaneously. Concerns over a bank's solvency will often trigger a bank run, and once it starts, it prompts more and more people to pull out their money leading to the demise of the bank and losses for customers that were unable to withdraw their money.

A most recent example was earlier in 2022 when sanctions were made against Russia because of its invasion of Ukraine. Several Russian banks experienced bank runs when they were removed from the SWIFT system for international payments. Over the last decade, we have seen bank runs in Sweden, the United Kingdom, Canada, China, Bulgaria, and Greece.

Brutal consequences were suffered in Cyprus during the 2008 crisis when the country needed to come up with 7.5 billion euros as part of a bailout package. If they didn't, the country's banking system would go bust. In March 2013, rumors started that the Cypriot government was considering a 'one-time tax' on bank deposits, taking money directly out of customers' accounts to fund this 'bailout.' Roughly 7.4 billion euros was taken from the two largest Cypriot banks' accounts overnight. They were replaced with worthless shares in the banks themselves. Wealthy savers had 47.5% of everything over 100,000 euros confiscated.

So the money in your bank account is not yours. It can be confiscated if the bank or government needs it to pay back their debts. Cyprus is not some oppressive third-world regime—it is a European Union country. How crazy does this sound?!

Don't think that could happen in America? Think again. In 2010 the Dodd-Frank Wall Street Reform and Consumer Act introduced a new safety net for banks called 'statutory bail-ins.' If there's another crisis, the banks can use your money to restructure themselves. They can steal your money! Without going into detail, the biggest banks have trillions of dollars worth of liabilities that would get paid before you do if the bank fails.

The 2008 financial crisis marked the beginning of trillions of dollars of bailouts for US banks. The Federal Reserve started lending money to banks in secret. They were literally increasing the total supply of dollars and flooding the banks with liquidity to save them.

Similarly, look at what happened during the COVID pandemic. The US government has thrown more than $6 trillion at the crisis. Where did all this come from? The Federal Reserve printed it! Trillions of dollars were created out of thin air. And eventually, when enough money was pumped into the economy, it started to work. The markets began to recover.

More money had been printed in 2 months than in the previous 250 years. Little of this money flowed down to the millions of Americans who were losing their jobs, their businesses, and struggling to pay for food and rent. The rich got richer, and the poor got poorer—again!

And as the US dollar is the world's reserve currency, everyone wanted dollars during the crisis. The Fed was printing money for the whole world, not just America. And everyone is paying for this with higher inflation, higher inequality, and higher taxes.

So the money in your bank account is not yours. You give away control of it. And the politicians and central bankers that do control it, do a poor job.

The timing of bitcoin's arrival was perfect. Just a month before Satoshi published his whitepaper, Lehman Brothers investment bank collapsed on September 15, 2008, as evidence of the broken banking system that led to the global financial crisis of 2007-2008.

It's not an evolution we need—it's a revolution in our money system. The rest of this chapter will explain what bitcoin is and how it can begin to solve the problems we face with current day-to-day fiat currencies.

So what exactly IS bitcoin?

Bitcoin isn't actually a coin at all—it's a computer program that creates and maintains data records in the form of a 'shared public ledger.' Your bitcoin is a piece of data that records your ownership of a certain amount of bitcoin. "Marco has 3 units of bitcoin" is essentially what a data record would show, for example. Cryptographic security methods are used to record your ownership digitally, making it impossible for anyone but you to access your bitcoin (more about that later).

The security of bitcoin comes from the decentralized nature of the technology. It's not controlled by any centralized organization or group of people. Control is spread across a whole community that collaborates to run the Bitcoin Network, with the data stored on thousands of computers worldwide. The technology that allows us to decentralize is called distributed ledger technology (DLT), which we commonly refer to as the 'blockchain.' Computers all around the world hold a full or partial copy of the data. So all the distributed computers are able to agree that "Marco has 3 units of bitcoin." This is why the data is now far more secure—it no longer sits in a single centralized location.

In today's banking system, if your bank's computer systems are temporarily unavailable, you have no access to your money during that time. In the UK in 2018, the Trustee Savings Bank experienced an IT migration failure that caused almost 1.9 million customers to be locked out of their accounts for several days. (4)

With distributed ledger technology, such problems cannot happen because the data is no longer vulnerable. If one of the 'nodes' in the network goes down, it doesn't matter because thousands of copies of the same data still maintain and verify the data records. If the bitcoin blockchain says that I own 3 units of bitcoin, all the different network nodes (or copies of the data) agree with this fact because they all have the same data that records this. I don't have to do anything else to prove that I own that bitcoin.

Centralized data also provides opportunities for malicious hackers to gain access to your bank's systems and drain your account of all its funds. Thankfully most banks will have guarantees and reserve funds to rectify such security breaches—but the fact is that crimes like this are possible, and they do occur. When a bank maintains a single log of your money in one place, this is a significant potential vulnerability.

Now imagine that instead of a single party holding a single log of your money, there are multiple different parties in different locations, each holding an identical log of your money. Every time you transfer some money into or out of your account, that transaction is shared with every one of the parties so that they can update their copy of the log of your money. Distributed ledger technology makes things infinitely harder for those malicious hackers to attack your data and steal your money.

In this way, the system of cryptocurrency is 'trustless'—it does not require trusted third parties. No intermediaries are required because banks or other financial institutions aren't needed to keep track of people's money. A government is not able to seize your assets. There is no 'trusted' third party that can interfere with any of the transactions, and the technology itself has removed the risks of failure or attack (more about that later).

This decentralization is the first 'big idea' of bitcoin. The second 'big idea' is about limiting supply.

I've mentioned already that bitcoin is a program. And this program defines all of the rules for the bitcoin currency—

how it can be issued, how it's stored, and how it's transacted. It also specifies that only 21 million bitcoins can ever be issued. No more. Ever. That rule is locked into the program. That's better than gold. No one really knows precisely how much gold exists, and although difficult, gold continues to be mined and added to the supply. So the gold supply is scarce, but bitcoin's supply is finite.

Unlike a dollar, one bitcoin will always equal 1/21 millionth of the supply. And it'll be yours forever. This is what makes bitcoin an excellent potential store of value. I say 'potential' because currently, we see large ups and downs with bitcoin's price. This current volatility means that bitcoin is a very poor store of value over the short term. Over the longer term, this will become less of an issue as adoption grows and price volatility starts to smooth out. We discuss volatility in more detail later on.

Now let's consider a government that's in a bit of a debt crisis. As I discussed earlier in the chapter, they can try and fix things by printing some more money. An unintended consequence might be that the country experiences higher inflation. Within the bitcoin ecosystem, it's not possible to create inflation because it's not possible to 'print' more bitcoin on demand. And there is no central authority that can change that rule.

Perhaps it's a weird idea that we can trust some software that specifies a rule like this. But we can. The bitcoin program is 'open source'—it's available for anybody to look at. Now I'm not suggesting that you or I are going to make a whole lot of sense from looking at the bitcoin code, but thousands of software engineers have, and there is consensus that the bitcoin program does what Satoshi Nakamoto described in his whitepaper. So we CAN be confident that only 21 million bitcoin can ever be created. And there are also rules for how that bitcoin is created and the speed at which it is created. There is complete transparency about how the bitcoin program works. That's most unlike our money system today with government-issued currencies. The government controls monetary policy, which means it can make changes to the rules of the money system. And such changes are not necessarily transparent or understandable in terms of their potential impact and how they might affect us as individuals.

So the cryptocurrency system is much more open and predictable than today's money system. Taken together with the distributed nature of the technology, cryptocurrency is a massive evolution, if not a revolution, in the way we think about money.

Originally, Satoshi Nakamoto intended bitcoin to be a payment method. In his whitepaper, he described it as "a new electronic cash system that's fully peer-to-peer, with no trusted third party." (5) He wanted it to be practical for small value payments. But bitcoin isn't a practical way to send small amounts to another party. The fees and delays of the Bitcoin Network make it impractical.

The fees don't depend on how much you are sending—they depend on how many other people want to transact bitcoin at that moment. All transactions are vying with each other to be processed. The original Bitcoin Network fees were fractions of a cent—but over the last couple of months, they have ranged between $1.25 and $2.72 per transaction. That's great if you are moving large amounts, but no good at all for small-value transactions. Further, when large numbers of transactions are waiting to be processed, the increased demand will drive up the average fee. During the buying frenzy late in 2017, fees spiked at one point to almost $60. (6)

The other problem with large numbers of transactions is the long wait time for transactions to be confirmed and added to the blockchain. Bitcoin can only process a few transactions an hour (currently around 10,000). Your bitcoin transaction could take anywhere from a few seconds to many hours to go through. This isn't practical if you are trying to buy an item in a store, for example.

Finally, in most stable economies, bitcoin's price volatility makes it impractical for payments. A tradesperson doing work on your house may quote you in bitcoin—but by the time you pay his bill, the value of that bitcoin could be wildly different.

These shortcomings have resulted in the primary 'use case' for bitcoin being as a store of value. Solutions for fast monetary payment systems are still emerging in the wider crypto ecosystem—but currently, there isn't anything to rival the processing speed and capacity of our credit card companies. Of course, it's just a matter of time.

How does it solve today's problems?

The number one solution offered by bitcoin is that it prevents governments and central banks from meddling with the money supply.

For people living in most mature western democracies, we experience around 1-2% inflation every year (although this is rising somewhat as I write). This means that you are losing about 2% of your wealth every year if it is stored in dollars—that's if you compare it to consumer prices. It's far more if you compare it to asset prices. Inflation steals your money, whereas bitcoin is a true store of value and a hedge against inflation.

Companies know all about the risks of holding cash balances too. Bitcoin is starting to make it onto public company balance sheets as a store of value to the tune of billions of dollars. The most well-known example is MicroStrategy, which was sitting on half a billion dollars of cash in the bank. With such poor returns from banks—this was a very poor use of capital. MicroStrategy's head Michael Saylor agreed with his board that they should move $425m into bitcoin to provide the return they wanted. Many, many companies are following suit.

Looking to the long term, some argue that bitcoin has a potential role as a global reserve currency. It's pretty much the only candidate for an asset whose supply cannot be altered for any government's advantage. It's genuinely neutral and impartial.

Under a bitcoin system, there would be no printing money, no massive bailouts, and no spending on taxpayers' behalf without their permission. There would be consequences for acting irresponsibly. Banks, corporates, and governments would have to be better capitalized. No more operating on debt ad infinitum.

You can still raise money for emergencies. The difference is that people would have to say, "Yes, we all agree to raise taxes for a year or increase our debt to get us out of this hole." Sure, there would still be politics and power, but a system underpinned by bitcoin would require more of a long-term focus and an end to the short-term giveaways to get elected. Bitcoin would be more democratic. It would be fair.

The second main solution offered by bitcoin is as a store of value worldwide. For some people, bitcoin is more stable, secure, and valuable than their own currency. The demand for 'hard' currency is typically off the charts where high inflation exists. The poor in these countries are not likely to have bank accounts—but many have a mobile phone—so they can buy bitcoin. Fewer than a billion people are now without a mobile phone, and this fast-changing statistic is helping to make bitcoin available to everyone worldwide.

I described El Salvador's adoption of bitcoin as an official currency as one such example in an earlier chapter. This was only possible with mobile phone 'wallets' and a network 'layer' built on top of the Bitcoin Network to enable fast and cheap payments (or fast and free as in the case with El Salvador's main technology partner). The 'Lightning Network' processes transactions 'off the Bitcoin Network' to avoid the problems of fees and delays. Transactions are netted off against each other, and the balances are 'settled' on the Bitcoin Network every so often.

There are still problems to overcome. For example, there are environmental concerns about energy usage. Bitcoin mining uses a lot of electricity. That's true. Bitcoin is using a rapidly increasing amount of energy at a time when we need to cut energy usage to counter the effects of climate change. That said, there are increasing examples of mining operations using renewable energy sources like solar, wind, or hydro. Further, it's not the case that all cryptocurrencies are as energy-hungry as bitcoin, as we shall see in a later chapter when I explain the mysterious 'mining' word.

Most people would concede that cryptocurrencies like bitcoin are here to stay. Even though the cryptocurrency market is in its infancy, the dollar value of the cryptocurrency market today is almost $900 billion (as of June 2022)—and that's when most major economies are experiencing sharp reductions in growth and the threat of a deep recession looms. Even at almost a trillion dollars, cryptocurrency represents just a fraction of the current global demand for money. No one really knows how much is out there, and many wide-ranging estimates exist. Taking one estimate of $150 trillion—cryptocurrency still only represents around 0.6% of the global demand for money. There is room for growth, for sure!

1.

"JP Morgan Chase reveals massive data breach affecting 76m households"
The Guardian, October 3, 2014
https://www.theguardian.com/business/2014/oct/02/jp-morgan-76m-households-affected-data-breach

2.

"Equifax to pay $700 million for massive data breach"
CNBC, July 22, 2019
https://www.cnbc.com/2019/07/22/what-you-need-to-know-equifax-data-breach-700-million-settlement.html

3.

"Capital One to pay $190M settlement in data breach linked to Seattle woman"
The Seattle Times, December 23, 2021
https://www.seattletimes.com/business/capital-one-to-pay-190m-settlement-in-data-breach-linked-to-seattle-woman

4.

"TSB lacked common sense in run-up to IT meltdown, says report"
The Guardian, November 19, 2019
https://www.theguardian.com/business/2019/nov/19/tsb-it-meltdown-report-computer-failure-accounts

5.

"Bitcoin: A Peer-to-Peer Electronic Cash System"

Satoshi Nakamoto, October 31, 2008

https://bitcoin.org/en/bitcoin-paper

6.

"Bitcoin Average Transaction Fee"

YCharts, 2022

https://ycharts.com/indicators/bitcoin_average_transaction_fee

5. YOUR #1 INTERESTS ARE SCARCITY + SECURITY

Why can't there be more bitcoin?

In the previous chapter, I mentioned that only 21 million bitcoins can ever be issued. There is no ambiguity about this—the 21 million supply cap is an integral feature of bitcoin and is fiercely defended by the bitcoin community.

To change the bitcoin program in any way, a 'fork' would need to be created to achieve this. The original program would continue to exist unchanged, and a new variation of the original program would exist in parallel. There have been hundreds of such forks created to offer 'improvements'—but in all cases, the bitcoin community has always rejected them and maintained its support for bitcoin and the Bitcoin Network.

The 21 million supply cap is why bitcoin was invented. It's what underpins everyone's perception of the value of bitcoin. Without this built-in scarcity, the value of bitcoin would decrease over time, just like the currencies we use every day. Bitcoin is the first finite asset in the world. Its monetary policy is built-in and unchangeable. As the world continues to suffer the effects of inflation, more and more capital will flow into bitcoin as a safe store of value. (1)

What is blockchain?

Back in the early days of the Internet, one of the first significant applications was email. The Internet was the technology needed to enable email, but as we know, it achieves a lot more than that for us these days. The same can be said about the blockchain. The technology has come into being to enable decentralized and secure cryptocurrencies to be created, but its application will be much, much broader than that in the future.

(Now, if you're not technical, take your time with the next couple of sections. It really is worth trying to understand how the technology is working. And I've kept everything at a conceptual level without, I hope, too much jargon.)

In essence, a blockchain is a 'ledger,' or a collection of records. These might be financial records such as payments, but they could be other sorts of data, too—like medical records, land titles, or shipments of goods and services. You can visualize the blockchain conceptually as 'blocks' linked together to form a continuous chain. Each block is like a page of the ledger, containing many individual records.

So why is this useful? Let's look at an individual block—it has three elements. First of all, there is the data stored in the block—for example, on the bitcoin blockchain, we would see transactions that contain the sender's address, the receiver's address, and the amount of bitcoin sent from the sender to the receiver. The second element is the address, or the signature, of the previous block in the chain. This way, all of the blocks are linked in a backward direction. Then finally, the third element is the address, or signature, of the current block.

These addresses, or signatures each block has to identify itself, are called 'hashes.' The term comes from the world of cryptography (the art of writing or solving codes) and means that each block has a unique identifier. This cryptography is used to secure the blockchain and enable secure transactions, which is why we use the term *crypto*currency.

If the addresses of any of the blocks were changed anywhere along the blockchain, then the chain would be broken. Everyone would be able to see that the data had been compromised. So the idea of chaining is the first concept in the security that the blockchain offers. But there is additional security that makes it very difficult to tamper with the contents of a block in the first place.

Imagine a malicious hacker attempting to change some of the data records stored on a block. When you change the contents of a block in any way, the technology forces a recalculation of the hash of the block itself. Even if you just changed a single letter or added a space, it would force the recalculation of the hash of that block. The hash wouldn't just change subtly—it would change completely. Therefore, that block would no longer be linked to the following block in the chain. The chain would be broken.

Therefore it's impossible to hide any data tampering because the chain will break as a result. The only way an attack could succeed is if the hash information in EVERY one of the following blocks could be recalculated and updated to re-establish the links between blocks before anyone noticed what was happening. This would be extremely difficult to achieve. But imagine for a minute that we've got a supercomputer that could make these changes at incredible speed—thousands of blocks could be updated almost instantly.

Despite having a capability like this, an attack would still be impossible because of the second concept in the security that the blockchain offers. This is to purposely slow down the creation of the addresses for each block—the hashes. You will have heard the term 'mining' in the context of cryptocurrency. The miners calculate all of the hashes that are needed to link the blocks of the blockchain together. So to slow down the creation of hashes, a 'puzzle' is introduced that miners need to solve before a new block can be added to the blockchain.

In practice, solving this puzzle before a new hash can be used means that it takes around ten minutes to add a new block to the blockchain. And this makes it practically impossible to hide your tracks if you attack and change any data on the blockchain because you could never quickly recalculate all of the hashes needed to re-establish an unbroken chain of blocks.

If that isn't enough, there is a third concept in the security that the blockchain offers—it is distributed. As explained in the previous chapter, centralized or single copies of data has its shortcomings. Blockchain is implemented as a network with thousands of identical copies of the blockchain data. There are currently over 15,000 members of the Bitcoin Network, or nodes (2), each with a copy of the bitcoin 'open source' software and the bitcoin blockchain data. If we configure the blockchain in this distributed fashion, we can compare copies of the blockchain data—and if copies don't match, then there is something amiss with the data. So when new data is added to the blockchain, there is a process called verification, where the nodes compare their data to ensure that it is identical. Once a majority of the nodes agree with the new data, then the new data can be added to the blockchain.

It's the process of mining that calculates the new hashes and verifies the calculations of other miners to maintain identical synchronized copies of the bitcoin blockchain data across the entire network. I hope that you can now see how secure this arrangement is. That computer hacker would need to attack over half of the nodes in the network and change the data simultaneously to stand a chance that the tampering would go unnoticed. This is practically impossible to achieve using any available technology we have today.

Finally, with regard to the security of blockchain technology, there is a system of cryptographic codes, or 'keys,' that is used to prove ownership of funds and initiate transfers of funds. Although the bitcoin blockchain is public and anyone can see everyone's bitcoin transactions—only the person with the correct key can access the bitcoin associated with a particular account. There is an oft-used phrase in the crypto world—"Not your keys, not your bitcoin." In other words, losing your keys means you no longer control your bitcoin.

Keeping your bitcoin safe is an important topic and will be explained fully in a later chapter.

What is mining?

Blockchain technology enables peer-to-peer transactions without the need for intermediaries. Banks, currency exchange agents, insurers, lawyers—the parties that currently may be 'helping' to complete a financial transaction in our current world—will all be charging fees for their services. As a result, we experience financial transactions that can be complex, expensive, and slow.

The security of blockchain technology I described in the previous section makes it possible to remove these 'trusted' third parties and evolve into much simpler, direct financial transactions. As an example, everyone will be familiar with the ever-increasing security demands of banks. Passwords, PINs, captcha phrases, security questions, 2-factor authentications via text, authorizations in phone apps, photos and phrases you have previously chosen. Layers and layers of security are being added to help keep the bad actors out of those existing aging financial systems. Blockchain provides a fresh start and an opportunity to remove all the increasing complexity that frustrates us.

On the Bitcoin Network, there are none of the trusted third parties that we see taking part in traditional financial transactions. Instead, all the transaction processing and verification required is performed by members of the bitcoin community—called 'miners.'

Miners each run a copy of the bitcoin program and maintain a copy of the bitcoin blockchain. They are competing with each other to solve a puzzle to be able to add the next block of transactions to the blockchain. Why do they do this? The miner that solves the puzzle first and adds the next block to the blockchain receives a reward—currently 6.25 bitcoin. In addition to the mining reward, the successful miner claims all fees associated with the transactions selected to make up the next block.

These rewards are built into the rules of the bitcoin program. So far, around 19 million bitcoin have been mined, and there are only 2 million remaining to be mined. Over time, the rewards to miners gradually decline, and the prediction is that the last bitcoin will be mined in 2140.

This system is called 'proof of work' and was designed to protect the blockchain from attack by slowing down the rate at which blocks can be added to the blockchain. The cryptographic puzzle miners have to solve isn't easy, and it takes time to generate a hash with the correct format that can be used as the address for the next block to be created. You need more than a laptop to mine successfully. Serious miners have racks of powerful computers with high-speed processors specifically configured to guess numbers to input to the puzzle—so called 'nonces.' The only way to mine a block is to guess nonces over and over until you happen to generate a hash with the correct format. It's a game of chance that is being played between miners.

Over time, miners have started to collaborate and share their processing power to generate more consistent rewards. These so-called 'pools' are now the default way mining takes place. There are just a few pools that control most of the processing power, and pools are continuously jostling for these top positions. Currently, around ten pools mine around 95% of all bitcoin blocks, and five of those mine the lion's share of 75%. (3)

What about the scammers and the hackers?

"Bitcoin has never been hacked" is a frequently made statement—although this is not strictly true. The Bitcoin Wiki (4) lists several bugs of varying severity, with the most recent being discovered in February 2019.

But nothing has compared to the bug discovered on August 15, 2010, where a hacker created an additional 184 billion bitcoins! (5) Thankfully, the hack was unsuccessful. The validation function across the whole decentralized Bitcoin Network enabled the malicious attack to be quickly discovered and removed. The bitcoin community fixed the bug and strengthened the network as a result.

The fact that the entire Bitcoin Network relies on consensus to validate transactions and to identify any malicious activity makes it the strongest computer network in history. If I own bitcoin, I like the idea that an army of supercomputers is protecting my investment.

While hackers have a close to zero chance of attacking the blockchain to steal your bitcoin, scammers are altogether more successful. A scammer will target the weakest part of the system—not the technology, but YOU. As in all other aspects of our financial lives, we must be hyper-alert to the possibility of interacting with scammers. They are clever and inventive people who will go to great lengths to get you to reveal your 'keys' to them.

The best way to protect yourself from scammers is to think slowly and logically when taking action with digital assets. Be skeptical and triple-check everything because the crypto world is largely unregulated and uninsured.

And always adhere to the one golden rule—you should NEVER share your private keys with ANYONE. I'll say more about the critical topic of keeping your keys safe in a later chapter.

Scary stuff? Well, yes and no. Over time, the crypto world will become more regulated and subject to controls that protect consumers, like in our traditional financial markets. But this will take time. Bitcoin is at the safer end of the spectrum of crypto assets and has already benefited from regulation that will assist more mainstream adoption.

While bitcoin may have been used in its earlier days to facilitate criminal activity, it's far from ideal because the transactions on the blockchain are public and available for all to see—hardly suitable for covering one's tracks! Criminals have shifted to so-called 'privacy' cryptocurrencies, like Monero, which does not enable anyone to audit another's transactions. But the favored currency of criminals worldwide? It's still CASH.

1.

"Is it safe? Is it safe?"

Ep.4 The Crypto Exposé Podcast, December 11, 2019

https://anchor.fm/thecryptoexpose/episodes/Is-it-safe--Is-it-safe-e9fetl

2.

"Reachable Bitcoin Nodes"

June 27, 2022

https://bitnodes.io

3.

"BTC Pool Distribution"

June 28, 2022

https://btc.com/stats/pool

4.

"The Bitcoin Wiki"

June 28, 2022

https://en.bitcoin.it/wiki/Main_Page

5.

"Bitcoin History Part 10: The 184 Billion BTC Bug"

Bitcoin.com News, February 28, 2019

https://news.bitcoin.com/bitcoin-history-part-10-the-184-billion-btc-bug

6. UP AND DOWN LIKE A YO-YO. RISKY?

Why is the price of bitcoin so volatile?

When you were first able to buy bitcoin, it would have cost you $0.003 per bitcoin. Imagine you had splashed out and picked up just $10 worth of the fledgling currency. You'd now be sitting on over $66 million (bitcoin is hovering around the $20k mark as I write).

And imagine what Florida man Laszlo Hanyecz must feel like—spending 10,000 bitcoins in May 2010 (worth $41 at the time) on two pizzas. This landmark moment was the first-ever purchase of a real-world item with bitcoin. Sadly, in today's money, those pizzas cost him $200 million!! No wonder May 22 is remembered as 'Bitcoin Pizza Day.' (1) Hanyecz's pizza purchase was significant because it was the first time the world saw that somebody thought bitcoins were economically valuable tools—starting a positive feedback loop.

Bitcoin has achieved a multimillion-fold price increase because of supply and demand factors. Let's look at supply first.

We've seen already that the bitcoin supply is capped at 21 million and that mining will continue until all 21 million have been 'minted.' This is the only way that new bitcoin can be created. By the mid-2030s, 99% of all bitcoin will have been mined, and at that point, the supply of new bitcoin will be a trickle.

In reality, the supply of bitcoins will likely fall over time because people lose their bitcoin. Or rather, they lose the 'keys' to their bitcoin while the actual bitcoin becomes inaccessible on the blockchain. As we shall see later, if you lose your 'private key,' you have lost your bitcoin. There isn't anyone who can reset things for you.

No one knows how much of all the mined bitcoin has been lost. According to the Wall Street Journal, around 20% of all bitcoin is lost and unrecoverable. (2) You will no doubt have heard stories of people who can't access hard drives that contain their private keys, or people that have lost passwords to access their digital wallets. Further, a large proportion of bitcoin is 'unavailable' because it is being held for the long term. The bitcoin that belongs to these wealthy 'whales' is not for sale!

So the pool of bitcoin available to be bought and sold right now is much smaller than we may have initially imagined. Chainalysis estimates that 60% of all bitcoin is being held for long-term investment (3), so after a further 20% that is lost, this leaves around 3.8 million bitcoin available to be bought and sold. As bitcoin becomes more scarce, the price of the asset is driven higher.

The other side of the equation is demand. This is an altogether different animal, and the changing pattern of demand is a major cause of the volatility in bitcoin's price that we see day by day, hour by hour, and minute by minute.

The factors that impact demand have changed over time. In the early days, it was all about awareness and familiarity. News about bitcoin traveled fast in a small tech-savvy community to create the early demand for bitcoin. Now that bitcoin is almost a household name and getting ever easier to buy and hold, demand is influenced by different factors.

As I write in June 2022, the macro economy has erupted big time over recent weeks. Inflation is increasing, interest rates are rising, equity markets are tumbling, the housing market is ready for a fall, and financial commentators are talking about a 30-50% chance of a global recession. During such times, investor confidence is at its lowest. Indeed, CNN

Business is reporting that the Fear and Greed Index is entering the territory of "Extreme Fear." (4) Predictably, money flows away from assets perceived to be more risky during these times—assets like bitcoin and other cryptocurrencies.

The crypto market is on the floor right now—there is little demand for perceived risky crypto assets. Nothing has changed about the technology and what it promises to achieve, and there is still as much innovation and development going on as there ever has been. But the broader macroeconomic picture shows that people and corporations have other priorities.

The demand for bitcoin is also further influenced, or compounded, by the media. Last weekend, the Sunday Times in the UK published an article titled "Is bitcoin just a giant scam?" You know how the media works these days. Once the market changes direction, so will the headlines.

Many figures in the existing financial establishment have voiced their distrust of bitcoin in the media. Warren Buffet said, "If you offered me all of the bitcoin in the world for $25, I wouldn't take it." JP Morgan boss Jamie Dimon said it was a "fraud" and would fire any employee trading it. The establishment always resists and rejects disruptive change. It's a threat.

Coverage of particular events has had dramatic effects on fledgling crypto markets. In 2014 a crypto exchange in Japan called Mt. Gox was handling 70% of the world's bitcoin transactions when it was hacked, and 740,000 bitcoins were stolen—at that time, worth hundreds of millions of dollars. Imagine the impact that this story had on consumer confidence in bitcoin! At the other end of the spectrum, last year, we saw significant movements in the price of a cryptocurrency called Shiba Inu due in part to tweets made by Elon Musk. All sorts of 'news' can impact the demand and, therefore, the prices of cryptocurrencies. Movements can be significant in either direction—and they can happen with lightning speed.

But as time passes, media coverage seems to have less impact. But crypto markets are still young, and they are very emotional places that under and overreact to all sorts of events. The conditions for an efficient market to function are still some way off.

One of the significant reasons for this is that information about cryptocurrencies and the crypto marketplace is very difficult to consume and interpret—there is a vast gap between the knowledge and experience of developers and the understanding of the investment community. Until people can witness and experience what the new technology can achieve, it's difficult to respond appropriately with buying and selling behavior. So the market is a bit 'skewwhiff' at the moment. It's reacting to some stuff that's understood, but not other stuff that's not understood. It's not an efficient marketplace. (5)

One final note is that the price volatility of this new technology also serves another purpose. If you look at the price of bitcoin over time, you will see clear cycles of price appreciation followed by a 'crash' in prices. But every time, the new low price is higher than the previous low price. Bitcoin grows stronger and scarcer in these down cycles. When bitcoin prices are going down, weaker investors are selling, and stronger investors are buying at cheap prices to build their existing holdings. This pattern repeats itself in all financial markets.

Despite the volatility over the shorter term, bitcoin has demonstrated strong growth over longer time periods. Bitcoin's compound growth per annum is over 150% on average over the past ten years—even though a down cycle may reduce the price of bitcoin by 70% or more! (6) For now, volatility is part and parcel of bitcoin's journey—and almost every other cryptocurrency, for that matter. But it will inevitably settle down as the technologies and the marketplace mature.

Isn't this all too risky?

Bitcoin may seem volatile if you live in a mature western democracy. Still, it starts to look pretty solid when your own currency is being devalued by more than 50% a year—like Argentina, for example. 73% of Argentines say bitcoin is the best form of savings for them in the current climate. Holding the local currency is financial suicide. (7)

If you live in a 'first world' country, you'll recognize some of the risks of money as we use it today. If you live in a country with a hostile government, then protecting your savings becomes a serious concern.

Bitcoin is no longer just owned by the 'enthusiasts.' Fund managers are now busy creating all sorts of cryptocurrency investment funds. I joined the first big wave of bitcoin euphoria in the second half of 2017 when many retail investors scrambled to own a bit of bitcoin. There was mass 'FOMO'—the fear of missing out. And this was accompanied by a crazy spike in the price of bitcoin that ultimately crashed again. Loads of small investors lost 50%, 60%, or maybe 90% of what they put in. I was amongst the unfortunate that got 'rekt' as they say in the crypto world. I was uneducated, and I paid the price.

It was too early. Bitcoin adoption didn't support those prices. Large price increases weren't sustainable, regulation was in its infancy, and the big institutions hadn't started to invest in crypto.

Despite losing over 80% of my bitcoin investment and various alternative cryptocurrencies, my belief in the technology and the ongoing innovation was unwavering. I held on tight, and eventually, three years later, bitcoin reached its previous end of 2017 high. Taking a long-term perspective based on the potential of this emerging technology is a much safer bet than trying to make short-term profits as the crypto markets move up and down on a daily basis.

It was the same in those pre-Google days when people were talking about the Internet "transforming our lives," and dot-com companies all had ridiculous valuations—before the bubble burst. The technology being developed today is promising another revolution for us all. And that revolution is a new cycle of boom and bust. Nothing has changed about the cyclical nature of technology innovation.

For long-term success, bitcoin can't just operate as it wishes. Countries have established mature legal, regulatory, and taxation frameworks for financial services, and bitcoin needs to co-exist alongside these. Regulation will help to create greater confidence around bitcoin. It paves the way for more institutional capital to flow into bitcoin. In turn, as bitcoin matures as an asset, we would expect to see lower levels of volatility and risk.

What is an asymmetric investment?

You may not feel comfortable moving your life's assets into bitcoin—despite it being the best-performing asset of the last decade. But holding just a little can make an enormous difference to the returns of a 'traditional' portfolio.

Imagine that you have a retirement fund holding 60% stocks and 40% bonds. According to a study by Bitwise Asset Management in 2020, holding just 2.5% in bitcoin could boost the cumulative returns of such a portfolio from 26.2% to 44.9%. And further, that the portfolio's overall volatility (or risk) would barely increase. (8)

If just 1% of your savings is allocated to bitcoin, your risk is very, very low. It would not be the end of the world if you lost it all. But that small bitcoin investment has the potential to multiply by 10 or maybe 100 over the next decade. We call this an 'asymmetric' return because the scale of possible returns far outstrips the chances of a loss.

Even fund managers are embracing bitcoin now for its abilities to diversify and potentially boost the returns of an investment. Fidelity recently announced that they were allowing customers to hold up to 20% of their retirement investments in bitcoin.

1.

"What Is Bitcoin Pizza Day?"

Coindesk, May 16, 2022

https://www.coindesk.com/learn/what-is-bitcoin-pizza-day

2.

"20% of All BTC is Lost, Unrecoverable, Study Shows"

Investopedia, June 25, 2019

https://www.investopedia.com/news/20-all-btc-lost-unrecoverable-study-shows

3.

"60% of Bitcoin is Held Long Term as Digital Gold. What About the Rest?"

Chainalysis, June 18, 2020

https://blog.chainalysis.com/reports/bitcoin-market-data-exchanges-trading

4.

"Fear & Greed Index"

CNN Business, June 15, 2022

https://edition.cnn.com/markets/fear-and-greed

5.

"Hieroglyphics and then some!"

Ep.5 The Crypto Exposé Podcast, December 17, 2019

https://anchor.fm/thecryptoexpose/episodes/Hieroglyphics-and-then-some-e9j217

6.

"Are cryptocurrencies a good hedge against inflation with their prices falling?"

The Business Times, June 29, 2022

https://www.businesstimes.com.sg/banking-finance/bt-explains-are-cryptocurrencies-a-good-hedge-against-inflation-with-their-prices

7.

"73% of Argentines Say Cryptocurrency Best for Saving in Economic Crisis: Survey"

Bitcoin.com, August 29, 2020

https://news.bitcoin.com/73-of-argentines-cryptocurrency-best-saving-economic-crisis

8.

"The Case for Crypto in an Institutional Portfolio"

Bitwise Asset Management, May 2020

https://static.bitwiseinvestments.com/Research/Bitwise-The-Case-For-Crypto-In-An-Institutional-Portfolio.pdf

7. SPEND $20. GET YOUR RAS GOING.

How do I buy bitcoin?

I've already described how the Bitcoin Network doesn't need trusted third parties and the benefits this brings. It exists entirely outside of the control of governments and financial institutions. Bitcoin is like the most secure bank in the cloud. No one can meddle with your money on the Bitcoin Network—except you.

Anyone can buy and hold bitcoin, regardless of nationality, political beliefs, or credit history. You don't need permission. You just need a mobile phone. And this means that most of the world's population can access bitcoin, not just those with a bank account.

In 2017, The World Bank estimated that 1.7 billion people do not have access to a bank account. (1) This statistic will have changed a little since then, but it provides a sense of the sheer scale of this exclusion from financial services around the world. One of the most significant benefits that bitcoin and other cryptocurrencies will bring is an inclusive financial system that exists in parallel and independently of today's traditional system.

Do you currently own any bitcoin? If so, you'll know that by owning some, you tend to pay more attention to the news and developments that relate to bitcoin and other cryptocurrencies. People who don't own any bitcoin, or other cryptocurrencies, pay much less attention. This isn't surprising because this is how our brains work. The Reticular Activating System is a brain function that brings things of interest to your attention—it acts as a 'gatekeeper' to focus our attention on certain things. Without our 'RAS' we would be inundated with constant sensory information. (2)

When you decide to buy a new car, you start seeing the model you like cropping up everywhere—your RAS is helping you pay attention to what's currently important to you. Similarly, if you dip your toes in the water and buy a little bitcoin, you are helping your RAS to pay attention in this area. It's an easy way to start gradually educating yourself about a new technology.

So my proposal is that you buy $20 worth of bitcoin. This will get your RAS going. You'll be paying attention. And you'll learn firsthand from the process of buying and storing your bitcoin.

In this chapter, I will cover everything you need to know to make your first bitcoin purchase. And even more importantly, how to keep your bitcoin safe. In the traditional financial system, a trusted third party keeps your money safe on your behalf—they have custody of your assets. In the world of cryptocurrency, you are responsible for the custody of your own assets. So keeping your bitcoin safe is a vital topic to understand.

You buy bitcoin on an 'exchange,' which is simply a marketplace for people who want to buy and sell cryptocurrencies. The exchange matches up the buyers and the sellers of each cryptocurrency. You will find bitcoin listed on practically all exchanges. It's the universal cryptocurrency—like the US dollar of the crypto world.

Using the biggest exchanges when buying and selling cryptocurrency is a good idea. Binance.com and Coinbase.com are currently the top players. These are the safest platforms to be transacting on. You can learn about the nuances of smaller exchanges later in your crypto journey.

Step one is opening an account. Reputable exchanges will require you to go through so-called KYC (or Know-Your-Client) validation, where you must submit a photo ID to prove your identity. It's pretty similar to opening a bank account. Typically, the more personal information you provide, the higher your transaction limits will be on the exchange. You'll just need the basic validation to get started. The process for every exchange is a little different, so choose one of the top three and follow through with the steps you're presented with.

Step two is to send some fiat currency to your new exchange account. The process for doing this differs slightly from exchange to exchange and from country to country also. I can link my UK bank account to Coinbase, so I tend to use that exchange for buying bitcoin. Once you've connected your bank account with your exchange, you can transfer $20 or the equivalent in your own fiat currency. I have found bank transfer to be the cheapest option, but it is also possible to send money to an exchange from a credit card account—again, what is possible will differ from country to country.

After a successful transfer, you'll see your balance displayed on your exchange account as "20 USD" or "20 GBP" or whatever your fiat currency is. The third step is to convert this to bitcoin. Coinbase makes this especially easy with a big "Buy/Sell" button. Once you click this, you enter "20" as the amount you want to spend, you make sure that bitcoin is selected as the 'Buy' currency (abbreviated as BTC, or sometimes XBT), and you make sure that the 'Pay with' option is your fiat wallet that contains your $20. Then press the "Buy Bitcoin" button.

Binance has a similarly straightforward process by clicking the "Convert" action that you see to the right of your fiat currency balance. Website design changes all the time, so things may look a little different to you. Take your time, stay calm, and use YouTube to find 'how to...' videos to help you if you get stuck.

And that's it. You are now the proud owner of $20 worth of bitcoin, and your account balances will have been updated to show something like 0.00101286 BTC. You will always see bitcoin balances with eight decimal places as each bitcoin is divisible into 100 million parts. Each part is the smallest unit of bitcoin, called a 'satoshi.'

Now you could stop right there. You've bought the bitcoin, and it's in your Coinbase account. But in actual fact, Coinbase is looking after the bitcoin on your behalf. It's just like having money in a bank account. This trusted third party is providing a custody service to you. So if you leave your bitcoin in your Coinbase account, there is a risk that you could lose it should Coinbase go out of business or its systems are maliciously hacked.

Coinbase is a giant company, so we might conclude that such risks are minuscule. Probably so. But during this current period of enormous economic turbulence, many large players in the crypto industry have faced difficulties. Suffice it to say that good practice after you buy your cryptocurrency on an exchange, is that you move it off that exchange and into safe storage under your own control. I will say a lot more about that in the next section.

But hang on! Didn't I say that cryptocurrency systems didn't need trusted third parties? Then why are we using services like Coinbase? Well, the reality is that we have a 'mixed' system right now, and we may always have some sort of mixed system with both centralized and decentralized components. I've chosen to suggest using a centralized exchange like Coinbase because it's easy. There are fully decentralized exchanges called DEXs—but using these can be a little more complicated.

How do I keep it safe?

I need to say a little bit about the cryptography employed by the Bitcoin Network. That may sound a little too technical to some readers. But worry not! I will try to cover just the stuff you need—not transition into technobabble.

The word 'cryptography' comes from the Greek 'kryptós' meaning 'hidden' or 'secret.' When you employ cryptography, the sender can encrypt a message using some sort of 'key,' and the receiver can decrypt the message by using a 'key' also. Cryptography is very much a part of how bitcoin transactions are created and stored on the Bitcoin Network.

We have already mentioned 'hashing,' which is one particular cryptography algorithm that enables us to generate the addressing and the structure of the blockchain.

But also cryptocurrencies use something called an asymmetric encryption algorithm, which basically means that we use 'keys' to lock up and unlock information that we send to each other. This enables me to create a financial transaction from me to you, which is totally secure along its journey. (3)

Let's say I'm moving 2.5 bitcoins from my account to yours. I need to create a blockchain transaction that essentially says something like this:

From:
0x89FbdB132D7ce9Aebb6A5be704Fb0a51aB7041Bc
To: 0xcFA58a0e12D14d2eFc4B1224d02Fd4F6A4d4F101
Amount: 2.50000000 BTC

You have shared your public address with me—this is where I send the bitcoin. I also select the public address of the account from which I want to send my bitcoin. Finally, I specify the amount to send. The transaction is then locked using my 'key.' This provides my authority to send the 2.5 BTC to you and ensures that no one can meddle with the transaction while it is added to the blockchain.

What's actually happening is that the transaction that's getting written to the blockchain is recording the fact that 2.5 BTC is no longer linked to my address—it's linked to your address. Nothing actually 'moves' from me to you. So once the Bitcoin Network validates the transaction, you will have control over this bitcoin by unlocking it with your own 'key.'

Now I've simplified this explanation a little to avoid going into detail about how the actual cryptographic method works. But there are two important principles to grasp.

A bitcoin transaction takes place between two bitcoin addresses—like the long alphanumeric strings you saw earlier. An address is generated from your 'public key' and can be openly shared with others so they can send bitcoin to you. It's like sharing an email address where you can receive bitcoin. It's possible to see how much bitcoin is being stored at a public address, but IMPOSSIBLE to steal unless you know the associated 'private key.'

Principle #1: You can share addresses generated from your public key—other people can send bitcoin to those addresses, but they cannot access any bitcoin that has been sent.

If you want to create a transaction that sends bitcoin from any addresses generated from your public key, you MUST have the 'private key' associated with this public key. The private key 'unlocks' the bitcoin at your public address and allows you to move it. Anyone who knows that private key will have full access to all of the bitcoin stored at any addresses generated by the associated public key.

Principle #2: If you don't hold your own private keys, your bitcoin isn't within your own control. NEVER share your private key with anyone, EVER.

Scammers have all sorts of elaborate tactics to get people to share their private keys, but there is NEVER any reason for you to share your private key. There is a well-known phrase popularized by Andreas Antonopoulos: "Your keys, your bitcoin. Not your keys, not your bitcoin." (4)

How do I store bitcoin?

Now that I've covered public and private keys, I can now talk about storing your bitcoin and the various options that you have. In actual fact, talking about 'storing' your own bitcoin is a bit of a misnomer because the transactions that record bitcoin ownership are always on the bitcoin blockchain. When we casually talk about where we 'store' our bitcoin, we really mean where we store the keys to our bitcoin.

Let's backtrack a little and revisit the $20 worth of bitcoin that we've bought on Coinbase or one of the other big exchanges. While your bitcoin is in your Coinbase account, it is being looked after for you. Your bitcoin is associated with a public address that has been created for your account, and Coinbase looks after the private key on your behalf.

Some people will prefer this arrangement because they don't need to worry about creating a 'wallet' of their own that would be used to store the keys to their bitcoin. But while the keys to your bitcoin sit on the exchange, your bitcoin could be lost, hacked, seized, or otherwise confiscated. Of course, Coinbase is a humongous and regulated organization. Therefore the risks of this are incredibly low— but it has happened, and smaller, less established exchanges will be more likely to suffer attacks.

There are two main options for people who want to take their bitcoin off the exchange and assume responsibility (and complete control) themselves. Both involve creating what is known as a 'cryptocurrency wallet.' And the most important purpose of such a wallet is to keep your private keys PRIVATE.

'Hot' wallets are so-called because they are apps that are connected to the Internet. Two bitcoin wallet apps that are currently popular are EXODUS (a very user-friendly app) and Electrum (for more advanced users). (5) (6)

Hot wallets should be used more for sending and receiving small amounts of bitcoin—much like you'd use a real-world wallet or purse. When you create a new wallet using one of these apps, you will create a new private key and a new public key that work together as a pair. Your keys will be kept safe within the wallet app and can only be accessed when you go through the security you have set up—typically a password and some form of 2-factor authentication like having a code sent to your mobile or using a 2FA app like Authy installed on your mobile.

Once logged into your wallet, you will be able to generate bitcoin addresses derived from your public key, that can be used to receive funds. You will also be able to send funds from any of your bitcoin addresses because the wallet app essentially 'signs' each of your transactions with your private key.

Hot wallets give you complete control over your keys. Their weakness is that they are Internet apps and, therefore, could potentially be hacked. But they are easy and convenient to use, and most people will be happy with the minuscule risk if they only have small amounts of bitcoin.

The most secure option is a hardware wallet or a 'cold' wallet. Instead of an Internet app, the wallet takes the form of a physical device, like a USB drive with a small screen. You can see what they look like by visiting their websites— the two dominant brands are Trezor (7) and Ledger (8).

Cold wallets are far more secure than hot wallets because your keys are not stored inside an Internet app. They are stored offline—inside your physical device—so hackers can't attack them.

Whenever you want to move your bitcoin, you need to connect your hardware device to your computer or mobile to 'sign' the transaction using your private key. This process of 'signing' with a private key is an encryption process. The transaction would be invalidated if anyone attempted to tamper with the signature. It's a bit like super-charged 2-factor authentication!

But what happens if I lose my hardware wallet? There's nothing to worry about in this instance. No one could access your hardware device without the password you created during setup.

When you set up your wallet, you create a backup passphrase (also called a 'recovery seed') of your private keys. If your hardware wallet is damaged, lost, or stolen, you can simply recreate your existing keys on a new device—thereby retaining access to your bitcoin. A best practice is to write down the passphrase (typically a sequence of 12 or 24 words) on paper and save this somewhere super safe. (9) Never record the passphrase anywhere digitally. You will create a backup passphrase in exactly the same way as a hot wallet, which you would also store safely on paper.

Recording your backup passphrase and keeping it safe is such an important step. You will have heard various horror stories about people who lost access to the bitcoin they bought years ago—maybe the device got damaged, or they forgot the passwords. With your passphrase securely hidden away, you won't be risking 'losing' your bitcoin.

Cold wallets should definitely be used when you have larger amounts of bitcoin or other cryptocurrencies. If you have more than $1,000 or so, I'd strongly recommend investing in a Trezor or a Ledger device.

A few further comments about hardware devices

You must buy your device brand new and direct from the manufacturer's website. Never buy a used wallet, and never buy from a 3rd party seller—like Amazon or eBay.

When you receive your device, ensure it has not been opened or tampered with—the package seal should be in place. Check the instructions carefully to ensure that the setup page URL is part of the company's official website.

Take your time setting up the device. Don't rush. The first step will typically be to install the latest version of the device's firmware. Then you will generate your recovery passcode and set up all the security for your device. Trezor and Ledger have very clear setup instructions. Their websites also have excellent educational videos that help you learn how to use their devices properly for receiving, storing, and sending cryptocurrencies.

If you lose or damage your wallet, you can buy a new hardware wallet on the BIP39 standard and enter your recovery seed into the new wallet. It doesn't have to be the same brand of wallet.

Remember, possession of your recovery passphrase is the same as possessing your private keys. Anyone that has your passphrase will own your bitcoin. Hide your recovery seed in a safe place and maybe make multiple copies.

Finally, start gradually. Move a very small amount of bitcoin to your hardware wallet first as a test. Make sure you are familiar with the process of moving bitcoin without making a mistake. Once you send bitcoin, the transaction is NOT reversible. So triple-check that the address you are sending to is correct. And make this a habit.

1.
"5 Facts About The World's Unbanked Population!
The Borgen Project, June 3, 2022
https://borgenproject.org/unbanked-population

2.

"Wake Up Your Reticular Activating System"

The Movement Paradigm, September 21, 2020

https://themovementparadigm.com/unlock-the-power-of-extreme-focus

3.

"Hieroglyphics and then some!"

Ep.5 The Crypto Exposé Podcast, December 17, 2019

https://anchor.fm/thecryptoexpose/episodes/Hieroglyphics-and-then-some-e9j217

4.

"Not Your Keys, Not Your Coins"

Stakefish, May 22, 2020

https://medium.com/stakefish/not-your-keys-not-your-coins-fad3d43c2713

5.

Exodus Bitcoin & Crypto Wallet

https://www.exodus.com

6.

Electrum Bitcoin Wallet

https://electrum.org

7.

Trezor Hardware Wallet

https://trezor.io

8.

Ledger Hardware Wallet

https://www.ledger.com

9.

The BIP39 List of 2048 English Words

https://github.com/bitcoin/bips/blob/master/bip-0039/english.txt

8. DOING NOTHING IS A GOOD OPTION

What is HODLing?

On December 18, 2013, GameKyuubi posted to the bitcointalk forum, "I AM HODLING." He was trying to say that he was committed to holding onto his bitcoin. But he was a little drunk, and his typo-laden post has given rise to the now-famous misspelling of "holding."

As we have already discussed, bitcoin can be an extremely volatile asset that responds to all sorts of news, true and false. This lack of predictability makes it difficult to make money over the short term—it's even a challenge for experienced traders with all of their technical analysis skills. For this reason, taking a long-term approach to investing in bitcoin is a far, far safer strategy.

If you believe that bitcoin's price will ultimately rise, the safer option is to buy bitcoin and then forget about it. DO NOTHING. Hold, or 'HODL' it for the long term and all of that day-to-day volatility becomes largely irrelevant.

There are, however, a couple of refinements to this 'do nothing' strategy. If you are human, you will no doubt worry about the price you pay when you buy your bitcoin. Will it go down tomorrow? Have I bought at the best moment? What if I wait a few days? (And you'll have similar worries if you come to sell.)

The first refinement is how you might buy and sell, depending on where we are in the overall market cycle. Is the outlook 'bullish' or 'bearish'? Are we close to the 'top' or the 'bottom'? This is relatively easy to know. Let's take a couple of examples.

As I write, bitcoin is sitting at around $20k. It has just suffered a rapid journey down to this level from the low $40k level and down from its all-time high of $68k. The market sentiment is one of extreme fear, and all sorts of market participants have gotten into trouble due to leveraged positions.

Leverage is where people borrow money to buy assets. Imagine those assets doing the opposite of what the borrower was hoping for, and they lose value. There is a point at which the borrowers are forced to sell their assets at a loss to pay off their loan. They have been 'liquidated.' Leverage is a dangerous game—not for you and me!

Right now, one of the largest lenders in the crypto industry, Celcius Network, has frozen all customer assets because of liquidation fears. If your money was with Celcius, you can't access it. As the fiasco unravels, the likelihood is that customers will pay the price for Celcius' 'degenerate' investment practices—they could lose every cent!

So things are most definitely 'bearish'—exceptionally so! "Have we reached the bottom?" people are asking. Regardless of what anyone may say, nobody can know if we have reached the bottom of this market cycle. It's impossible to guess. Impossible to divine with any analytical tool. But we can't be anything other than near the bottom. So it's the BEST time to buy. Sure it could go lower, but it's irrelevant because if you HODL, you'll be making plenty of money during the journey to the next all-time high bitcoin price. All you need is a bit of confidence to buy when no one else is buying.

The converse is also true. Most people will buy bitcoin when the market is buoyant, and prices are going up. They 'FOMO in' (fear of missing out). The market sentiment is one of extreme greed, and there is a lot of leverage in the system (people borrowing to invest). This is a 'bullish' scenario. Everyone is talking about the 'top.' "How high will it go?"

Just as you will never time the bottom, you will never time the top either. No one will know when prices will start to reverse. So, again, you don't even try. As the market heats up and becomes more euphoric, you should NOT be buying. You will be paying too high a price if you get caught up in the enthusiasm to buy. Your choice is either to HODL, or if you want to realize some profit, this is the time to sell. And perhaps this is the hardest thing to do—to sell in a rising market. But if you push greed to one side, you will see this as the sensible option.

So the first refinement is all about knowing 'roughly' where we are in the cycle and buying and selling accordingly. The second refinement is about *how* to buy and sell. Dollar Cost Averaging.

Imagine we are around the bottom of the cycle, and it's a great time to buy bitcoin with your $1,000. Now you could simply go ahead and buy $1,000 of bitcoin in one go—and you'll do just fine because you're buying low in the cycle. However, a better approach is to buy smaller amounts regularly over a period of time. As a strategy, this reduces the impact of short-term volatility by averaging things out and ensures that you don't overpay because you happened to buy when bitcoin zoomed up in price for just a few hours. Or imagine if bitcoin continued to move down in price after you bought it. Buying in smaller amounts regularly over a period of time would enable you to secure a better average price. Spend some time Google-ing "Dollar Cost Averaging" and actually put the approach to use. Remarkably few people do—all too often, people are in a rush to 'get in'—and it's often not the best thing to do.

Regular investing in this way works well over the long term. For example, if you have $600 a month available to buy bitcoin, buy $150 every Monday at 10 am. Or, even better, you could buy $20 every single day at 10 am. Many platforms will manage this for you automatically. You could easily move your dollars once a month to Coinbase and set up an instruction to buy $20 of bitcoin daily on autopilot.

The same strategy should also be used when selling. Don't sell all at once. Sell in smaller amounts regularly over a period of time to reduce short-term volatility. Also, if you sell in a rising market (before the 'top'), you will achieve a better average price.

One final thought. As I said earlier, selling when the market is going up is very, very hard to do. It could (and probably will) go higher. But I can tell you that most people who hold out for the 'top' end up losing out on a good selling opportunity because they just can't face selling when bitcoin is on its way back down into the next 'bear' market. I've found it much easier to sell, say, 70% of what I have and let the other 30% go a bit higher. When it does, I sell another 70% of what I have and let the remaining 30% carry on. Of course, eventually, the price will correct, and I can choose to sell the remaining fraction at a lower price or HODL for the next cycle. "Not financial advice" as they say, but I've found it to make sense.

A HODL approach with Dollar Cost Averaging for investing and withdrawing funds saves you from the emotion that would otherwise accompany your decision-making. You'll have heard the term FOMO—the 'fear of missing out.' Many smaller investors have rushed to buy bitcoin as the price started to rally. They don't want to 'miss out.' But if you are holding for the longer term, say five years or more—the price you buy at and the timing of your purchase aren't so relevant. Stick to buying little and often—regardless of what is going on with the price action.

Over time, you'll begin to see the patterns. You'll know that a price drop always follows a big rally. Celebrate when the price falls. This is when nervous smaller investors typically sell because they fear losing more money. The larger investors, the so-called 'whales,' will be BUYING MORE at this time because, from their vantage point, bitcoin is currently 'on sale'!!

What else could I do?

It's beyond the scope of this book to go into depth about other investment strategies that involve cryptocurrency. It's not sexy—but HODLing should undoubtedly be the core strategy for a beginner (and probably all more crypto-educated folk as well).

Although you can happily keep your bitcoin in 'cold' storage as I described above. There are other ways to put your bitcoin asset to work.

One option you might consider is to keep your bitcoin in a crypto bank—like NEXO. Currently, NEXO will pay you a minimum of 4% pa on your bitcoin and 5% pa if you lock it up as a 30-day term deposit. There are other ways you can use the platform to increase your savings interest rate further. HOWEVER, platforms like NEXO are not regulated like banks, and your money may not be protected to the same extent. The big players advertise that your money is insured. But it's probably unclear if you would get any of your funds back if they were facing a liquidation crisis—like Celcius is right now!

You get relatively high levels of interest paid to you because these crypto banks can lend out your deposit at even higher interest rates. You need to satisfy yourself that a crypto bank isn't lending in a 'degenerate' fashion to achieve unrealistic returns—and that isn't easy to ascertain. So something to consider, perhaps, but don't put all your eggs in one basket, as they say!

Another popular way to earn 'interest' is by 'staking' your crypto. This is possible on many of the newer blockchains where users of the network 'pledge' their crypto to the network to help the blockchain validate transactions. In exchange for staking, you get rewards, often in the form of the cryptocurrency you have staked. Polkadot, Cardano, and Ethereum 2.0 are all examples.

The returns are variable and change between platforms. Any numbers I publish here would be out of date by the time you read them, but I'd encourage you to do your research, and you'll see numbers that far outstrip any bank interest you might be 'enjoying' right now. Of course, these strategies also carry risks, so you must always do your own research, and have confidence in the project and technology you are investing in.

One next step in your journey might be to dig into the whole area of decentralized finance or 'DeFi.' That might sound boring, but I promise you, the innovation happening in this space right now is EARTH-SHATTERING! You can tell this excites me—sufficiently to start writing about DeFi in my follow-up book to this introductory text.

9. TO BOLDLY GO...

What is the future for bitcoin?

It is still extremely early in the development of bitcoin. Don't own any? You have not missed the boat by a long way. There is a long journey ahead lasting many years, and the demand for bitcoin needs to grow significantly so that current volatility settles and the currency becomes more stable.

You can happily spend a few hours reading people's guesstimates about the future value of bitcoin. In my opinion, if you believe that the trends I've identified in this book are at all likely—then every single prediction I've read would be a gross underestimate of bitcoin's future value. Once it takes its full place at the table of the world's financial system, a single bitcoin could be worth tens of millions of dollars. So you're not too late. You are super early. With an exciting ride ahead.

We've already seen El Salvador adopt bitcoin as legal tender, as well as the Central African Republic. Countries whose economies are in such a state that they have nothing to lose.

But as first movers, they are innovators and could accumulate power and wealth through bitcoin if their experiments go well.

Other governments are holding large quantities of bitcoin as well as large corporations. It's estimated that they own 8% of all bitcoins—around $32 billion at the current bitcoin price of about 20k. MicroStrategy holds the lion's share of 129,000 BTC, and Elon Musk's Tesla comes in second with 43,000 BTC. (1) These holdings are evidence that bitcoin is being held as a 'reserve asset' of preference over others like cash or gold.

As well as a strong reserve asset, bitcoin is a perfect candidate currency for global trade. Because it's neutral and non-political, the Bitcoin Network could become the ultimate global settlement layer of the next evolution of our digital economy—replacing the US dollar. In 2021, billionaire US fund manager Stanley Druckenmiller issued a stark warning that the dollar could cease to be the predominant global reserve currency within 15 years! (2)

While experts and bitcoin supporters are eager and confident that the crypto oozes potential to handle global trade and support global financial markets, bitcoin would be an unlikely choice for today's governments. It would be like returning to the gold standard in that a government wouldn't have much control over its economy, and forces outside its control would determine the value of money. A central bank would no longer be able to regulate the economy by controlling the money supply as needed—and the government's monetary policy would be at the mercy of uncontrollable forces.

Yet reserve currencies have always changed throughout history—each tied to the world's biggest trading nation at the time. It's not going to be the US dollar forever, and now you can see many reasons why not. It will happen. The debt creation in 2020 could be the tipping point.

Right now, about two-thirds of countries anchor their currency against the dollar. The dollar makes up over 60% of all known central bank foreign reserves, making it the de facto global currency. The euro comes in next at just 20%. (3)

If the US economy suffers, the whole world suffers. When the Fed prints money, it devalues the entire planet, which isn't a sustainable course of action. Money printing will eventually bring down the dominant global currency.

China and Russia know what's going on. They are stockpiling gold to ensure they have a stronger store of value in anticipation of the dollar's decline.

China is doing everything it can to internationalize its currency, the yuan. It is becoming much more common in global trade. But the yuan is still a fiat currency that can be manipulated and controlled just like the dollar. Additionally, any shift in this direction of power towards China is likely to unsettle global politics further.

Bitcoin offers an apolitical choice. It doesn't choose sides between the US and China. It isn't tied to a single economy. It can't destabilize the whole planet at once. Bitcoin as the world's reserve currency is undoubtedly possible—but there's a long journey to get there.

A future world of surveillance and intervention?

The successor to the dollar will almost certainly be natively digital. Governments know this, and every central bank in the developed world is now looking at building a digital currency.

It's a frightening prospect that the government would have programmable, trackable money. They could track every one of your payments, maintain a detailed financial profile of you and control how you spend your money. They could block transactions, freeze cash, and take your money without permission. They could issue more money and distribute it however they like. A government could control this form of money like never before.

How about money that has an expiration date if you don't spend it? What if it can be used for certain things but not others? How about controls over the payments that businesses make through programmable incentive/tariff structures? The issues of traceability and programmability raise major ethical issues. This technology opens the door to *personalized* monetary policy. Think about that for a moment. A government could segment individuals, groups, and communities in all sorts of ways and apply different incentives/controls to how money is used.

This is fiat currency on steroids and paves the way for a dystopian, totalitarian society.

I know this sounds like my imagination is going wild, like I'm going too far. But please do your own research about these government-controlled digital currencies and draw your own conclusions. They're called CBDCs—central bank digital currencies—and they're already here. (4)

China has developed Digital Currency Electronic Payments (DCEP), a digital payment version of China's fiat currency—the yuan. The currency had a moderately successful trial at the Beijing's 2022 Winter Olympic Games but still carries out localized testing ahead of a full-scale rollout. By the end of 2021, almost $10 billion has been transacted using the digital currency, and over 140 million people have opened electronic wallets for the digital yuan, or 'eCNY.' (5)

Job almost done in China! The perfect tool for a communist government to control its citizens. China is also making huge inroads into economies that are massively underbanked but where people have cell phones—Nigeria is a good example. China's influence in Africa could be huge. Imagine China having unlimited power and surveillance over half the world's population.

These CBDCs are the antithesis of bitcoin—no freedom, no privacy, no decentralization. They are 'spyware' currencies. Once people understand what is going on, they will clamor for an alternative solution for their money. Bitcoin provides us with an alternative. The technology will evolve around bitcoin to create an entire economy to rival the broken fiat currencies—digital or not.

So is the future bright?

With regard to crypto technology, I firmly believe our future is bright beyond our imaginations.

Our younger generation will power the rise of a new financial system to replace the old broken one. Wealth is going to change hands. The Millennials are going to lead the way. I know this—my kids are Millennials. They talk about crypto. It excites them because it's an integral part of their digital world, and they see opportunities for wealth creation. Young people are buying small fledgling currencies no one has heard of, NFTs that no one knows about. New communities of young innovators are growing fast.

Maybe it doesn't matter if you're retired and have your pot. Chances are that you'll be able to ride out your devaluing currency. But perhaps you could do better for your descendants and future-proof your portfolio?

The Millennials and Generation Z groups will grow up in this new world. But this book is mainly speaking to those in the middle. Those who are suffering right now at the hands of the current financial system and those that will lose out if they don't embrace the opportunity of an emerging alternative.

Those approaching pensionable ages know that their economy can no longer fund everyone's retirement fully. People are living much longer, and governments have been spending pension reserves. There's nowhere near enough money to pay out what is promised. I knew 20 years ago that a government pension wouldn't be worth anything by the time I retired—the writing has been on the walls for years. Private pension providers will have to meet impossible demands as the performance of bonds and cash wrecks the performance of assumed to be 'safe' portfolios.

The world will begin to change as crypto-savvy young people increasingly gain influence in our corporations and governments. Crypto expertise will become mainstream. In much the same way as the development of the Internet, we will begin to see new products, services, businesses, and jobs that never previously existed.

In the early 1990s, few people would have ever imagined that thirty years later, we would be sharing our worlds with each other through social media, ordering every conceivable product or service from the comfort of our armchairs, and traveling the world with apps that help us plan our routes and book our buses, trains, and planes. Similarly, few people will be able to imagine crypto's impact over the next thirty years. I'm sure it'll be the stuff of science fiction today.

It'll all happen seemingly slowly and gradually over time. Massively powerful technology and unparalleled levels of innovation have already been created, with most of the planet's population unaware of where this could be going. But people are slowly waking up to these new technologies and innovations and seeing the inevitability of a different money system in the future. Eventually, the balance will be tipped, and money will flood from the fiat system into bitcoin and the entire crypto economy.

Any transition to this future will likely be rocky and disruptive. Nations will lose some of their existing power and will obviously be doing everything they can to hold onto it. We see this already with bans on bitcoin activity or tight controls and regulations. But bitcoin can't be wiped out. Governments realize this. Whatever the future looks like, bitcoin will inevitably coexist on the global stage.

1.

"Govts, companies own 8% of all Bitcoins worth $46 bn in the world: Report"

Business Standard, May 26, 2022

https://www.business-standard.com/article/markets/govts-companies-own-8-of-all-bitcoins-worth-46-bn-in-the-world-report-122052600874_1.html

2.

"The demise of the dollar? Reserve currencies in the era of 'going big'"

The Financial Times, May 25, 2021

https://www.ft.com/content/408d4065-f66d-4368-9095-c6a8743b0d01

3.

"Why the US Dollar Is the Global Currency"

The Balance, March 16, 2022

https://www.thebalance.com/world-currency-3305931

4.

"CBDCs: A Monetary Highway to Hell"

Hustle Escape, 2022

https://www.hustleescape.com/cbdc-advantages-disadvantages

5.

"China's CBDC Has Been Used for $9.7B of Transactions"

CoinDesk, November 3, 2021

https://www.coindesk.com/business/2021/11/03/chinas-cbdc-has-been-used-for-97b-of-transactions

10. THE INNOVATORS ARE BUSY RIGHT NOW

This book is primarily about bitcoin. It's a gateway into a much bigger world of technology that is fast developing. Small teams of people across the globe are busy collaborating on new innovative ideas for putting crypto to use and delivering value to all sorts of different communities. Some of these will become proper fledgling businesses in a new 'Web3' economy, and some of those will emerge as the next Amazon, Facebook, or Google.

Yet, this world is largely underground and unfamiliar to most people. It operates differently. Anonymous developers collaborating across geopolitical boundaries to bring new technology to all sorts of different communities with common interests or characteristics.

I want to use the final part of this book to give you a brief taste of this emerging world. And I'd like to issue a warning to you also. Should you start to explore and research the broader world of crypto, GO SLOWLY. Please don't rush into anything—especially where it may involve you parting with your hard-earned fiat money.

You are early in crypto's development, so there isn't any rush. The territory is largely unregulated, so you are 100% responsible for your own investment decisions with little recourse if things turn sour. Make your objective one of learning first, and only invest when you feel that you really understand what's going on and how things work.

There are many different parts of the crypto world beyond bitcoin. They all relate and overlap, but each has its own communities, culture, and language—Altcoins, NFTs, DeFi, metaverse, and gaming are some examples.

By the way, the main job of this book is now complete—so skip straight to the conclusion if you feel like you've had enough tech speak for now. You can always return to this chapter later if you are hungry for more. The following sections also serve as a very brief introduction to the content of my next book, "*What is this crypto thing?*"

10.1 ALTCOINS

The term 'Altcoin' generally refers to any cryptocurrency or token that isn't bitcoin. Looking on CoinMarketCap today (September 10, 2022), I can see that there are 20,921 cryptos listed. Many smaller, newer cryptos will not yet be listed.

In September 2020, bitcoin represented over 70% of the value of the entire crypto market. Today, two years later, that figure has dropped to 39%. So you can see that the space is fast growing and changing. Each crypto or 'coin' has its own purpose, features, and benefits, and many compete for dominance in their particular niche. Of course, the majority of these will fail over time, and only a few will succeed in taking their place in our future day-to-day lives.

So will bitcoin ever be replaced by one of these other cryptos? Probably not. So far, any attempts to provide an 'improved' alternative to bitcoin have failed miserably. Bitcoin has established itself as the most powerful computer network in the world—it has proven itself to be resilient and secure. As a store of value, it's the only show in town, and it does this job supremely well. Other cryptos do other things. And there are an endless number of 'other things.'

Ethereum

The most well-known altcoin is called ether, and it runs on its own network—the Ethereum Network. It is quite a different beast from bitcoin altogether. It's not trying to be money. Ethereum is programmable, which means you can build things on it like you build an app on the Internet.

Ethereum was the idea of a 19-year-old Russian-Canadian computer scientist Vitalik Buterin. His white paper described a blockchain that could do far more than just record transactions—it can run code, host apps, store data, and do all sorts of computational work.

One significant feature of the Ethereum blockchain is the idea of smart contracts or mini-apps that live on the blockchain. Smart contracts follow specific rules and can move money, data, or other assets around in accordance with these rules. The contracts have 'addresses,' and you can send them commands to make them carry out their programmed actions for a small fee.

You can see an example of a contract by going to the Ethereum Blockchain Explorer at https://etherscan.io and searching for the contract address 0x7ef865963D3A005670b8F8Df6aed23e456FA75e0. You will be able to see the code executed to create a unique digital artwork I bought last year.

There are many potential uses for smart contracts. They can enable lending, borrowing, and trading without using banks and other financial intermediaries. They can function as legally binding contracts that support business agreements without requiring lawyers. They can record the purchase and ownership of real-world assets like real estate and works of art. They have applications in gambling, gaming, auctions, crowdfunding, voting, healthcare, smart technology, artificial intelligence—and the list goes on and on. Just like bitcoin, smart contracts cut out intermediaries.

Here is a simple example so that you can see the power of a smart contract. A sports fan wants to bet $10 that her favorite team will win the championship. She sends $10 worth of ether, the cryptocurrency that powers the Ethereum network, to a smart contract's address together with the name of the team she wants to bet on. Once the championship has ended, the contract checks with a sports news service like ESPN to see which team has won. Successful gamblers would receive their winnings automatically, and the smart contract would retain some money as profit for the creator of the smart contract.

Ironically, smart contracts aren't really smart—they execute their code like robots and so always operate precisely as they are programmed. Anyone can see the code that they run, and no one is able to mess with their behavior once they are published on the blockchain. In this way, smart contracts are decentralized applications (or 'DApps') that enable 'trustless' transactions to take place—users don't need to place their trust in any people or third-party organizations. You interact with these DApps in just the same way as you use web-based applications—except the backend code is run on a blockchain.

Smart contracts are not unique to the Ethereum Network, but this is where this technology all began, and innovation continues at a blistering pace. The blockchain was designed to operate much like bitcoin, using a 'proof of work' system for validating new transactions. But the success and growth of the network have resulted in exceptionally high transaction fees at times when the network is most busy.

At the time of writing, Ethereum has just transitioned to a new method of validation called 'proof of stake.' This has been a significant transition project to the new 'Ethereum 2.0' Network. One of the outcomes will be reducing the bottlenecks the original network experienced, which led to high transaction fees.

'Proof of stake' is a more energy-efficient mechanism than 'proof of work' since it uses less computing power to secure a blockchain. The change also brings further improvements in speed, security, and sustainability.

Like the Bitcoin Network, the Ethereum Network looks set to play a major role in the future crypto landscape. Accordingly, I'd say it'd be a pretty safe bet to invest in a little ether to go along with your bitcoin—a perfect second toe in the market. Again, that's not financial advice—only my own view based on the dominance of these two technologies.

Other Alts

Taken together, bitcoin and ether account for almost 60% of the total crypto market by value. The next 'top 10' Altcoins account for a further 25% or so, and the remaining 20,909 Altcoins account for the remaining 15%. You can see how a few 'large cap' coins dominate the market. Generally, these will be somewhat safer investments than the 'mid cap' and 'micro cap' coins. Of course, there will be some amazing future success stories hidden amongst the thousands of tiny fledgling cryptos, which may produce returns of more than a hundred times the original investment—sometimes even much more. But finding these opportunities is not an easy or risk-free pastime!

I'm going to provide a very brief overview of some of the 'top 25' Altcoins so that you can see how they differ from bitcoin and ether.

Solana and other Layer 1 networks

As I outlined above, Ethereum was originally designed using a 'proof of work' system of validating transactions, and its popularity resulted in a slow and expensive network. Solana was one of the networks seeking to provide a faster and cheaper alternative to Ethereum and used 'proof of stake' validation from the outset. The Solana Network offers the same programmable functionality as the Ethereum Network but was designed to rival the speed of existing payment providers like Visa and Mastercard.

The network's SOL token is used to enable the 'proof of stake' validation system and as the currency used to pay fees associated with transactions and smart contracts.

Other so-called 'layer 1' networks that rival Ethereum also feature in the top 25 cryptos—Binance Smart Chain, Cardano, Polkadot, Avalanche, and Near Protocol. Such alternatives have proliferated, and each attracted enthusiastic communities of developers and users. Perhaps it will be less important in the future which networks we choose to use, but we will need to build 'bridges' between them.

Dogecoin, Shiba Inu, and other meme coins

By 2013 there was widespread speculation in a whole range of available cryptocurrencies. Two software engineers, Billy Markus and Jackson Palmer decided to create their own payment system purely to poke fun at this speculative market. In December 2013, they launched what is regarded as the first 'meme coin' and indeed the first 'dog coin'!

You've no doubt heard of Dogecoin. The face of the 'coin' was taken from the Doge meme, created from a viral photo of a Shiba Inu dog. Despite its satirical intent, the crypto quickly amassed strong popularity and price appreciation. Dogecoin has become the 10th largest cryptocurrency, with a market capitalization of over $7.5 billion. Yet it remains very volatile. Tweets by Elon Musk that reference the meme or the coin have had a significant impact on Dogecoin's price.

Dogecoin is promoted as the "fun and friendly Internet currency." Many merchants accept the currency for online payments and it's also used to tip content creators on some social media platforms. Many people also HODL Dogecoin as an investment—although this is a good example of a cryptocurrency where you might just as quickly lose money as you gain it.

Other meme coins have followed Dogecoin—over 200 in total. Shiba Inu is currently the 14th largest cryptocurrency, with a market capitalization of almost $6 billion. Others are mostly dog themed and tiny in market capitalization compared to the 'big two,' though. Examples are Baby Doge Coin, Floki Inu, Poodl, Cake Monster, Banano, Woofy, Kitty Coin, Catbonk, Donkey, and Chihuahua Chain, to name just a few.

Uniswap, PancakeSwap, and other decentralized finance protocols

Large centralized exchanges like Coinbase and Binance can be used for buying and selling many of the larger cryptocurrencies. But smaller, less well-known cryptos are often not listed.

For example, let's say you are interested in buying some UFO Gaming tokens. This crypto is ranked on CoinMarketCap.com as the 362nd largest crypto with a market capitalization of just over $50 million. It's too small to find on Coinbase or Binance, so you must hunt for it elsewhere. A smaller centralized exchange like KuCoin trades UFO Gaming, and so does a decentralized exchange like Uniswap.

Uniswap is the leading decentralized exchange. It isn't owned and operated by any single entity, and it enables the trading of tokens on the Ethereum Network through smart contracts. Unlike the centralized exchanges that work by matching up buyers and sellers to complete a trade, Uniswap uses a very different method to enable trades to take place that does not require any intermediaries.

When I was writing this section, I started to explain how Uniswap actually works. I realized that I was disappearing down an entirely unnecessary rabbit hole. So I have moved this explanation into my next book. Let's keep this as simple as possible!

As well as using Uniswap as a platform to exchange one crypto for another, you can also buy Uniswap's own token, UNI. This goes up and down in value like any other crypto. It was created as the governance token of the Uniswap platform—UNI holders that hold over 1% of the total supply of tokens can submit development proposals and influence the future of the exchange. Regardless of how much they hold, all holders of UNI can vote on such proposals.

The code for Uniswap's smart contracts is all 'open source,' and several 'clones' have been launched as a result. One successful platform is SushiSwap—also on the Ethereum Network, with a few differences from the original Uniswap.

PancakeSwap is a hugely successful clone of Uniswap but runs on the Binance Smart Chain Network instead of Ethereum. It offers fast and inexpensive trading, all facilitated by its own CAKE token.

Chainlink and other utility coins

Chainlink is a blockchain-based technology that contributes to the operation of smart contracts. As I mentioned above, the outcome of a smart contract may depend on the outcome of a sports fixture. The outcome could depend on all sorts of data—temperatures, currency rates, published statistics, and events that take place. This external data could be anything at all, so long as it comes from some agreed data provider or 'oracle.'

Chainlink works with data providers to create a huge marketplace that smart contracts can access. The 'oracles' providing the data will charge a small fee, and the smart contracts requesting the data will pay this fee. Payments are made using Chainlink's token LINK. Data providers can purchase LINK and deposit it within the Chainlink system as collateral for compensation to data subscribers should incorrect, or no data be delivered. Essentially, more LINK equals more trust. This technology is regarded as one of the most important in the development of smart contracts.

Many other so-called 'utility' coins are enabling all sorts of blockchain activity. Monero is an example of a cryptocurrency that offers privacy as its utility. It uses technologies that obfuscate transactions to achieve anonymity. Unlike other 'public' blockchains I have mentioned above, it is impossible to see sending and receiving addresses, transaction amounts, or address balances on the Monero Network.

As you might guess, Monero is increasingly being used in illicit activities such as money laundering, transactions in darknet markets, and crypto attacks of all sorts. You can also imagine that the United States Internal Revenue Service (IRS) is interested in breaking the privacy algorithm that Monero uses so that transaction data can be visible to them, and they are actively incentivizing tech firms to assist them.

Cryptocurrencies are being developed with all sorts of different utilities in all sorts of different niches. While we would recognize some as currencies, others confer other benefits such as ownership, governance, membership, trust, reward, and entertainment.

Stablecoins

As we have seen with bitcoin, price volatility is one reason why it makes a poor cryptocurrency for payments. A cryptocurrency fit for payments must focus on stability rather than growth. This is what stablecoins do. They maintain a fixed exchange rate with a fiat currency like the dollar or the euro. Stablecoins are designed to be stable!

The most commonly used stablecoins are 'pegged' to the US dollar. They are designed so that their exchange rate with the US dollar is always 1-to-1. They achieve this using one of two primary methods—it's super important to understand the difference, as you shall see.

Before the United States abandoned the gold standard in 1971, every US dollar was 'backed' by the equivalent amount of physical gold. Therefore governments could not devalue the currency by deciding to print more money. The first way stablecoins achieve their stability is for every crypto dollar to be 'backed' by a real fiat US dollar held on deposit somewhere as collateral for the crypto.

USD Coin, or USDC, is an example of this type of stablecoin issued by CENTRE—a joint venture between Coinbase and Circle. The cryptocurrency is backed by US dollar-denominated assets held at regulated and audited US financial institutions. The international accounting firm Grant Thornton LLP issues monthly attestations on the reserves backing USDC.

This 1-to-1 backing provides the confidence that 1 USDC will always retain its value of 1 US dollar. This enables crypto transactions to take place with a stable currency instead of a more volatile currency like bitcoin, for example. This is especially important for payment applications and occasions when low-risk crypto assets need to be held without exiting to a fiat currency.

The most popular stablecoin in use is Tether—another example of a stablecoin pegged to the US dollar by maintaining assets in its reserves equivalent to the dollar value of Tether in circulation. Tether publishes its own quarterly attestation, but this is not the same as an audit from an independent external accounting firm like USDC provides. This lack of transparency and authenticity of the reserve is often called into question, and gives rise to some controversy around Tether. Accordingly, USDC is perceived as a safer and more transparent asset.

Now let's look at the second method in which stablecoins can achieve their stability—using an algorithm rather than a physical reserve of real-world assets. This type of stablecoin typically relies on two tokens—the stablecoin plus another token that backs the stablecoin—and a smart contract (the algorithm) controls the relationship between the two. This is a clever alternative to needing real-world assets to provide backing for the stablecoin. But it all went horribly wrong in the case of TerraUSD's UST stablecoin.

Like all cryptocurrencies, the price of UST will vary based on supply and demand. But the objective of a US dollar stablecoin is to remain at a price of $1.00. So, when the price of UST rises to, say, $1.01, the Terra protocol allows users to exchange $1 worth of the second token, LUNA, for 1 UST.

When the trade is made, the $1 worth of LUNA is 'burned' (permanently removed from circulation) and 1 UST is 'minted' (created just like a new physical US dollar is printed). The user can then sell the new 1 UST at its price of $1.01 and make a profit of $0.01. This doesn't sound much, but it is an excellent quick profit for a trader making a very large transaction.

As more users take this opportunity to make money, the amount of UST in circulation increases. This inflation of the currency brings the price back down to $1.00, where the opportunity to make a profit disappears.

The reverse happens if the price of UST drops to, say, $0.99. A user can buy 1 UST for $0.99 and then exchange that for $1 worth of LUNA. The trade burns the 1 UST and mints $1 worth of LUNA. Deflation of the UST token continues until the price returns to $1.00 again.

There had been criticism of this algorithmic approach to maintaining the $1 peg of UST. In response, Do Kwon, the main man behind UST, set up Luna Foundation Guard in February 2022 to support the stablecoin's peg by buying as much as $10 billion in bitcoin as a collateral asset. (1)

If this all sounds a bit complex, stick with it for a while so that you figure out what is going on. It's really clever—and is an excellent example of the innovation happening across the crypto space.

Sadly though, this clever innovation wasn't perfect, and on May 7, 2022, the price of UST started falling on all trading platforms around the world. Within 48 hours, its value had dropped to $0.35, and the LUNA token was worth almost zero. UST investors had lost nearly $45 billion in just a few days. (2)

These were extreme circumstances, and Do Kwon's explanation was that the algorithm was unable to mint LUNA at the pace required to maintain UST's peg with the US dollar. The drop in UST's price caused widespread panic that the stablecoin was failing, and a mass sell-off resulted in the complete collapse of the protocol.

There's plenty more that you can find out about this event and the reasons it occurred. I hope my brief summary here helps you to see that it can be very hard to predict how new crypto 'products' will perform in our complex and fast-changing global economy. Even protocols regarded by investors as relatively 'safe' may not turn out to be what they seem.

Tokenization

Tokenization is the process of converting something of value in the real world into a digital token that a blockchain application can use. This includes tangible assets like gold, real estate, and art—or intangible assets like voting rights, ownership rights, and content ownership. (3)

This process can seem a little baffling, so I will take a real-life example. Pablo Picasso's 1964 painting "'Fillette au béret" has been tokenized. Instead of having a single owner, ownership of the painting has now been divided into 4,000 'Art Security Tokens,' enabling someone to own a fraction of the Picasso rather than the entire painting. Although the original artwork is stored safely in a vault somewhere, these digital tokens are automatically recognized by the courts as legal chunks of the painting that can be traded as the owner sees fit. (4)

The technology of blockchain tokenization is providing broader access to assets that are typically hard to buy and sell, and smaller investors are able to hold assets that they otherwise wouldn't be able to afford to buy outright.

Another example of tokenization is the idea of a central bank digital currency (CBDC)—already introduced in the previous chapter. A CBDC is essentially a tokenized fiat currency. For most people, there might be small gains in efficiency and security to be had as money movement becomes a bit easier—but tokenization is unlikely to change the structure of an economy. A tokenized fiat currency is still a fiat currency where the government ultimately controls the money, and the money's value is based only on faith in the country's government.

1.

"Algorithmic Stablecoins: What They Are and How They Can Go Terribly Wrong"

CoinDesk, May 16, 2022

https://www.coindesk.com/learn/algorithmic-stablecoins-what-they-are-and-how-they-can-go-terribly-wrong

2.

"Old vs New 'Revival' LUNA Crash: Which Costed Terra Community More Loss?"

Analytics Insight, May 31, 2022

https://www.analyticsinsight.net/old-vs-new-revival-luna-crash-which-costed-terra-community-more-loss

3.

"What Is Tokenization in Blockchain?"

Cryptopedia, August 12, 2021

https://www.gemini.com/cryptopedia/what-is-tokenization-definition-crypto-token

4.

"The Art Of Tokenization: How A Picasso Painted Itself Onto The Blockchain"

Forbes, April 27, 2022

https://www.forbes.com/sites/martinrivers/2022/04/27/the-art-of-tokenization-how-a-picasso-painted-itself-onto-the-blockchain

10.2 NON FUNGIBLE TOKENS (NFTS)

I commonly come across the perception that NFTs are just 'pictures.' Sadly, the richness of this area of the crypto landscape is poorly understood outside of the 'inner circle.' In honesty, I'd need to write a whole book to explore the full scope and utility of NFTs. As with Altcoins, my goal here is simply to offer a taster. And there's no better place to start than talking about those 'pictures' and explaining exactly what an NFT is!

NFT artwork

Let's start with Cryptopunks. Pay a quick visit to https://opensea.io/collection/cryptopunks, and you will see a collection of 10,000 pixel art images that were launched in June 2017.

Had you wanted to buy one of these at any stage during the past week, you'd have parted with a minimum of $87,000. That's right. $87,000 for a tiny piece of pixel art!! But wait for it—on March 11, 2022, one Cryptopunk sold for $7.5 million.

What's going on? Why are people parting with such vast sums of money for a Cryptopunk? Let's start at the beginning.

NFT is an abbreviation for non-fungible token—a record on a blockchain that is associated with a specific and unique digital or physical asset. In the case of Cryptopunks, there are 10,000 unique pieces of pixel art—each with its own combination of distinctive traits and features—and there is an NFT associated with each of these recorded on the Ethereum blockchain. If you own the NFT, then you are the owner of the associated piece of pixel art.

This compares with a cryptocurrency token, which is a fungible token. Every token of a particular cryptocurrency is identical and interchangeable rather than unique.

The limited collection from Lava Labs was one of the first NFT projects on the blockchain. When it was originally created, or 'minted,' as they say, there was no cost to anyone that claimed one, except the Ethereum transaction fee for the minting transaction itself—at the time, this was just a few cents. Those that had heard about the project early secured a Punk.

The rarity of each Punk's characteristics differs—for example, there are 9 alien-type Punks compared to 6,039 male Punks, and sale prices reflect these sorts of differences. However, the community of Punk owners remains strong, and few sales take place. This digital scarcity, the cachet of Cryptopunks being one of the very first NFT collections, and belonging to this community drives the incredible sale prices.

Collectors are drawn by the #1 NFT asset. Many owners display their Punk as their main social media avatar—Punks have become the first digital status symbol!

Of course, Punks were first, and an avalanche of NFTs followed, all vying for attention in a fast-emerging marketplace. Predictably, most of these copycat projects failed to gain any traction. Those that have succeeded do have one critical factor in common—a strong community. The best example of this is undoubtedly the Bored Ape Yacht Club—a collection of 10,000 cartoon apes launched by Yuga Labs in April 2021.

Bored Apes have captured everyone's attention in the NFT space. The artwork was originally minted for a price of 0.08 ETH (that's $112 in today's money), and over the last seven days, those same NFTs have changed hands for anything between $98,000 and $234,000. That's quite an appreciation in price over just 18 months!

The value of the collection was originally based in a super strong community, but Apes have gone much further than Punks ever have. Two further NFT collections were created and given free to Bored Ape Yacht Club NFT holders—Bored Ape Kennel Club and Mutant Ape Yacht Club. These NFTs sell for upwards of $10,000 and $21,000, respectively.

More than anything, though, holding a Bored Ape NFT means that you belong to that community. It's an elite membership card that grants access to exclusive online forums and meetups all over the world. 'Ape Fest' was organized for Bored Ape holders in June and included performances from Eminem and Snoop Dogg. Several high profile celebrities now hold the NFTs, further boosting interest in the collection.

Where people place value on belonging to a community like this, they are less likely to sell their NFT. Those that are listed for sale can command incredibly high prices. Bored Ape Yacht Club #8817 was sold by Sotheby's auction house for $3.4 million in October 2021. (1) The most unique Bored Ape, according to website rarity.tools, is #7495—it has never been sold.

The founders of Yuga Labs continue to innovate to add value to holders of Bored Apes. They have already launched a crypto called Ape Coin, which will be the primary currency in 'Otherside'—the metaverse they are building. All Bored Ape holders were given 10,000 Ape Coins each at launch—for free. Even at today's depressed crypto prices, this is a gift of over $57,000 to each NFT holder.

In the physical world, Bored Apes are partnering with fashion brands, restaurants, and Universal Music has even signed a band comprising Bored Ape Yacht Club members! The project has demonstrated how NFTs are so much more than just a little digital picture. Over just 18 short months, Bored Ape Yacht Club has redefined what can be achieved in the NFT space and established itself as possibly the number one 'blue chip' NFT to hold.

NFTs in gaming and metaverse

Video gaming has been with us for over 40 years now. Today the complexity of game design can cost tens and even hundreds of millions of dollars. The costs of game design are starting to outstrip Hollywood budgets. Indeed, the entire video gaming sector is now larger than the movie and music industries combined. NFT technology is set to fuel more explosive growth in the sector.

In-game assets, such as characters, objects, environments, and indeed all sorts of physical and virtual items and properties, can be created as NFTs. NFTs that can be bought, sold, and transferred from one gaming environment to another.

The starting point for all of this was CryptoKitties—a popular virtual cat breeding game released in November 2017. (2) CryptoKitties are collectible NFTs you can buy and sell using ether. The game enables you to breed two of your cats and produce a kitten that inherits some of the features of each parent cat. An entire 'economy' has grown around the game and fans have written all sorts of guides explaining how to breed kittens and make money—from assets that don't exist in the real world!

Crypto gaming has developed significantly over the past five years, and there has been an explosion of 'play-to-earn' games. The most successful example so far is Axie Infinity—inspired by Nintendo's Pokémon series. The game enables players to collect cute monsters called Axies and then battle with other monsters. (3)

New Axies can be created through breeding, enabling players to build strong teams for battles. As NFTs, they are tradeable on marketplaces—one Axie has sold for a staggering 300 ETH (currently $415,000). Winning battles earns you the in-game currency AXS, which is tradeable on the Binance exchange. So you can convert your winnings to hard fiat currencies.

The game became a phenomenon, especially in the Philippines, to generate additional income. But over time, the economics of the game have not been sustained, and players have left the platform as the play-to-earn benefits have become less enticing.

The development of crypto gaming still has a long way to go. The big gaming studios like Sony, Microsoft, and Nintendo remain on the sidelines for now.

This relatively early stage of NFT application in crypto gaming is also reflected in metaverse projects. It is early days for environments like Decentraland and The Sandbox, but this looks like the next evolution of our web experience. Metaverses will be 3D virtual worlds where we will spend our time working, socializing, and playing. We will be able to visit art galleries, attend concerts, and visit exotic locations—only our imaginations will limit what we will be able to do and achieve.

You will undoubtedly have heard many established brands talking about their metaverse intentions. Facebook has renamed itself as 'Meta,' and other big players like Microsoft, Apple, and Amazon will likely be at the forefront of metaverse innovations. However, in 2022, we can only see the first primitive examples of this technology.

NFTs are programmable

NFTs can be much more than just pictures—they can be programmed to create dynamic digital assets. A simple example of this is a digital artwork that has royalty functionality.

In the traditional world, once an artist has sold an artwork, they won't receive any more money, no matter how valuable the artwork may become. If an artwork is created as an NFT (or an NFT is used as proof of ownership of a physical work of art), then an ongoing 'royalty' to the artist can be programmed in, and the artist will receive this payment every time the artwork is sold.

This idea works for more complex applications like royalties on video games, where publishing a new game requires working with many different external contractors such as musicians, special effects artists, and character designers. There may be hundreds of complex royalty contracts in place for a single game—and managing all of these is an immense challenge that requires extensive documentation and accounting resources.

Xbox has simplified things greatly with a blockchain-based royalty settlement system, where royalty contracts have been transformed into smart contracts. Instead of taking 45 days to calculate royalty payments, this work can now be done in minutes. (4)

Another example of using programmable NFTs would be to reform the archaic process of voting, where we queue up to put a mark on a ballot paper, and then these are counted by hand. This process will always be open to fraud or failures, especially in 'democracies' that are somewhat less than democratic, where tactics such as vote rigging and intimidation are employed.

The technical process is straightforward in principle. The government would issue a voting token to everyone eligible to vote in an election—an NFT. Each voter then sends their token to an address representing the person they want to vote for. There's not much more to it than that. There aren't any possible counting errors, interfering with the results isn't possible, and there's a complete audit trail of the voting that can be verified.

Few countries have embraced any kind of digital voting because of the practical implementation challenges. Estonia is one trailblazing exception, though. Since the March 2019 parliamentary elections, more than 40% of ballots have been cast using an online system. (5)

The main challenge of online voting is deciding who should get a voting token in the first place. Estonia enables citizens to verify their identity by issuing electronic ID cards that are tied to their smartphones. Over 90% of Estonians have these secure IDs, which makes online voting possible.

Despite progress in Estonia and pilots in countries like Switzerland and Columbia, widespread adoption feels like a long way off. The only example so far of a blockchain-based NFT voting system has been developed by a 12-year-old boy in the Philippines, but perhaps this isn't the ideal political arena for a successful trial! (6)

Through these two examples, you can see that NFTs are actually programmable digital assets. The application of this technology is still very much in its infancy. Over the coming years, we will likely see NFTs used in all sorts of settings— entertainment, fashion, real estate, publishing, financial services, healthcare, advertising, and travel— to name a few.

Generative art

Finally, I've added a little section about 'generative' art, simply because I love it! This is where art meets science— unique works of digital art created as the output of a computer algorithm. Art Blocks is home to many of the major digital artworks that have been created so far, and you can spend many hours browsing through the vast number of collections. (7)

The artists use their programming talents to create algorithms that spawn unique works of art that exhibit the aesthetic qualities they are striving to achieve. Every time the algorithm executes, a different, random, unique work is produced.

A great example of the results of a particular algorithm is 'Fidenza,' created by the artist Tyler Hobbs. (8) Each output features structured curves and blocks, but the variety in the organization, size, and color of these give rise to many extraordinarily unique artworks. Another hugely successful collection you might browse is 'Ringers,' by Dmitri Cherniak. (9)

Each algorithm will be relentlessly tested to ensure it will generate artworks that adhere to the aesthetic and variety of output that the artist is seeking. But what is remarkable is that no one will see the final artworks in a collection before they are bought! A 'minting' event takes place online, where a limited number of artworks are created at the very moment they are bought.

Fancy a Fidenza? You can pick up a cheap one right now on OpenSea.io for $132,770. Or if you can't quite manage that, how about a Ringer for $76,068? Of course, the more 'interesting' works that the algorithms have produced will cost a little more. So perhaps it would be better to set your budget above $200k?

The original mint price for Fidenza was 0.17 ETH (currently $235), and for Ringers, it was 0.1 ETH (currently $138). Those who spotted the potential of these collections early have made extraordinary investments, as Fidenza and Ringers are now regarded as top 'blue chips' in the world of NFTs.

1.
"Top 11 Most Expensive Bored Ape Yacht Club NFTs"
Crypto Times, March 30, 2022
https://www.cryptotimes.io/most-expensive-bored-ape-yacht-club-nfts

2.
CryptoKitties
https://www.cryptokitties.co

3.
Axie Infinity
https://axieinfinity.com

4.
"Xbox will now use blockchain for gaming rights and royalties"
Techradar, December 16, 2020
https://www.techradar.com/news/xbox-will-now-use-blockchain-for-gaming-rights-and-royalties

5.
"Estonia leads world in making digital voting a reality"
Financial Times, January 26, 2021
https://www.ft.com/content/b4425338-6207-49a0-bbfb-6ae5460fc1c1

6.
"How a 12-year-old boy developed an NFT voting platform for the Philippines"
Forkast, November 19, 2021
https://forkast.news/12-year-old-boy-nft-voting-platform-for-philippines

7.
Art Blocks
https://www.artblocks.io

8.

"Fidenza" by Tyler Hobbs

https://www.artblocks.io/collections/curated/projects/0xa7d8d9ef8d8ce
8992df33d8b8cf4aebabd5bd270/78

9.

"Ringers" by Dmitri Cherniak

https://www.artblocks.io/collections/curated/projects/0xa7d8d9ef8d8ce
8992df33d8b8cf4aebabd5bd270/13

10.3 DECENTRALIZED FINANCE (DEFI)

I've dedicated the final section of this chapter to talking a little about decentralized finance, or DeFi. Just like NFTs, I'd need to write a whole book to explore the range of technologies and applications that are emerging in this area. The topics and examples below are far from exhaustive, but I hope your interest is piqued.

WARNING: Because it is so new and unregulated, the Defi landscape is full of risk. If you choose to participate, do so with great care and take those familiar words to heart: **You shouldn't invest more money than you can afford to lose.**

On the other side of the coin, DeFi investments can promise such extraordinary returns that you may feel they are worth a 'flutter.' However seductive a particular project is, I'd strongly suggest that dipping your toe into DeFi should be considered an alternative to an 'investment' in a lottery ticket.

The crypto 'banks'

Many of the largest centralized crypto firms offer familiar banking-type services like deposits and withdrawals, savings, lending and borrowing, and investing in a wider range of instruments and markets. Despite their size and offerings, they are NOT part of the current regulated banking system. Despite firms like Nexo and Coinbase replicating many financial services on the blockchain, these only mimic those provided by banks. They lack the full range of services and integrations, and the safety, security, and protection regulated banks offer their customers.

These crypto 'banks' may become a future part of our regulated financial services markets, but for now, they do provide a very useful 'bridge' between the world of traditional finance and the world of crypto. Customers are able to deposit their own fiat currency and exchange these for a whole host of major cryptocurrencies.

Deposits also typically earn interest that is much higher than traditional banks offer. For example, the best rates I can currently find for instant access savings with a traditional bank are around 2% per annum. If I convert my fiat currency into a stablecoin like USDC and deposit this with NEXO, I will earn 8% per annum. This difference is rather attractive! But of course, there are some risks involved that you need to be cognizant of. There are risks associated with the cryptocurrency that you convert your fiat currency into, and there are risks associated with the crypto 'bank' entity itself.

Just this spring, crypto 'bank' Celsius Network collapsed, and thousands of investors are out-of-pocket to the tune of around $4.7 billion. (1) Unlike the traditional banking system, there are no protections that safeguard investor funds. Celsius was investing in other platforms offering similarly high returns to keep its business model afloat and ultimately got into difficulty when its own investments ran into trouble.

So crypto 'banks' are interesting places to explore and potentially use to diversify some of your savings. However, you now know they don't offer the same safety and protection as your traditional bank.

Yield farming and liquidity pools

Earning interest on your crypto deposits in a crypto 'bank' is relatively straightforward, but it's not all you can do in the DeFi space by a long way. For me, yield farming was the next opportunity I explored. This is essentially lending, or what is called 'staking,' your crypto in exchange for interest or other cryptocurrency rewards.

Various yield farming platforms will take your staked crypto and then lend this out to innovators who need crypto, or 'liquidity,' to launch and grow their projects. Compound Finance is one of the big players in this market, and a visit to their website will show you the various rates on offer to lenders and borrowers.

You can also contribute your 'liquidity' to decentralized exchanges like UniSwap and PancakeSwap. They will use your money to facilitate the process of swapping between pairs of cryptocurrencies. For example, you can buy BUSD-BNB LP tokens, and you will currently earn 6.24% per annum on PancakeSwap.

This will no doubt sound like gobbledygook to you! I'll give you a quick example, so you get the idea. Let's say you have $100 that you are holding in the BUSD US dollar stablecoin. You convert half of this to the BNB cryptocurrency, and then you buy some BUSD-BNB 'liquidity pair' or LP tokens on the PancakeSwap platform using your $50 of BNB and your $50 of BUSD. These tokens are then deposited, or 'staked,' on the PancakeSwap platform. The platform uses this 'liquidity pool' to enable trading to take place efficiently between the BNB and BUSD tokens. Whenever a trade takes place on the platform, you, as a liquidity provider, will receive a small proportion of the fees received from the trade.

This is actually quite a complex area of DeFi, so don't worry if this still sounds like gobbledygook. Something for later, perhaps. Like crypto 'banks,' yield farming platforms are not risk-free—but the rewards can be pretty exceptional when staking some of the more esoteric cryptocurrencies.

Other passive income protocols

Many crypto products have been created with smart contracts to offer passive income. One of the most well-known was the Anchor Protocol, which provided lending and borrowing based on TerraUSD's UST stablecoin. The platform was regarded by investors as super-safe and offered a return to lenders of almost 20% per annum. Over $14 billion had been invested in the Anchor Protocol, but users fled the platform as the UST stablecoin started to collapse on May 7, 2022.

The consequences for investors in this 'safe' protocol have been dramatic. The collapse of UST and the Anchor Protocol has given rise to all sorts of discussions about the risk and sustainability of this and other similar protocols.

Yet passive income products continue to evolve—some die without a trace after a few months, and others continue to perform well. Critics shout "Ponzi!" while faithful supporters laud the talented developers that have made them rich. Passive income DApps in the DeFi space are controversial, risky, and also somewhat irresistible.

I must admit that this is one area where I have 'invested' small amounts of money. I certainly would not recommend any particular protocols to readers of this book. However, for educational purposes only, I would suggest looking at DRIP. This is a relatively simple protocol you can read up about and get a feel for what these DeFi products are all about. (2)

More esoteric products

The current economic downturn has created harsh conditions for investors in new crypto projects. Innovators are doing their best to generate returns and maintain loyal communities that support their work. We are seeing many projects morph from their original objectives into new and different directions that will reward investors. One of the NFT projects I've invested in provides an excellent example of this—Generous Robots. (3)

In crypto, it's generally regarded to be a good thing if you can buy into a project right at the very start—before anything is traded on an exchange. Investors at this early stage can see profits of 20, 50, or even 100+ times their original investment. The problem is that allocations in these projects tend to go to the bigger players, and small investors find it difficult to participate in any meaningful way.

The idea of Generous Robots was to raise money by issuing a collection of NFTs, which would enable it to become a 'big player.' Healthy profits could then be made through meaningful investments in new projects and then distributed to the holders of the NFTs. This way, small fish can invest in new projects efficiently—just like the big players.

So I bought a few Generous Robots NFTs. And then the economic downturn struck. Far fewer projects wanted to raise capital in this climate, and Generous Robots no longer had a robust model for generating income for its investors.

The Generous Robots project needed to change direction to stay alive and maintain the support of its NFT holders. The NFT artwork was improved, a new utility token was introduced, staking of NFTs was possible in return for the new token, and the token could be used to unlock benefits from various partner projects.

The ideas of Altcoins, NFTs, and DeFi have all come together in this one project. Will it succeed? I do hope so, as the founders are super talented and have devoted enormous time and energy to the project. But like many crypto projects in the space right now, it feels a little rudderless and makes frequent changes of direction to try and navigate the harsh economic environment. The outlook for such projects is not bright.

Now is not the time for esoteric projects and products. Now is the time for crypto innovators to focus on the fundamentals of the technology so that they are solid and ready when economic growth and investment begin again. This is why this book has focused on bitcoin and given the briefest of introductions to other parts of the crypto world.

Bitcoin shows us what a solid, successful project looks like, and it'll be around for a good time to come.

1.

"From $25 billion to $167 million: How a major crypto lender collapsed and dragged many investors down with it"

CNBC, July 17, 2022

https://www.cnbc.com/2022/07/17/how-the-fall-of-celsius-dragged-down-crypto-investors.html

2.

DRIP Network

https://drip.community

3.

Generous Robots DAO

https://generousrobots.com

CONCLUSION (BEGINNING)

I hope more than anything that you've started to understand what this bitcoin thing is all about. This has been a beginner's guide, so there's much, much more to be said about bitcoin and the entire crypto space—but my objective was simply to support your first steps.

I also hope I've encouraged you to take the plunge and hold a small amount of bitcoin. So that you'll no longer be a 'no coiner.' If you've decided not to enter the bitcoin world at this time, that's totally fine too. What's important is that you made an informed decision.

Now that you've reached the end of this introduction, you'll understand several important ideas:

- Bitcoin is early in its development. It's a volatile asset but will become more stable as adoption continues.
- Bitcoin is just one of over 20,000 other cryptocurrencies. The crypto market is u.

with innovation and creativity right now—just like in the early days of the Internet.

- Countries have started to make serious moves to use bitcoin as part of their overall monetary system—especially more unstable economies suffering from very high inflation.

- Bitcoin demonstrates how a cryptocurrency is a next evolution from today's 'fiat' currencies. It has a fixed total supply and avoids the problem of inflation that today's money-printing governments are creating.

- The Bitcoin Network provides a 'trustless' secure alternative to the current financial networks that rely on 'trusted' third parties, who all take their 'cut' of your money.

- The universal availability of bitcoin technology means that many of the world's population that are currently 'unbanked' can now participate in the financial system.

- With a bit of care, it's easy for an individual to buy and hold bitcoin now. It's a solid first step into the whole world of crypto.

- HODLing and DCAing are important strategies to employ when investing in crypto (or any investment asset).

- Bitcoin has the potential to be used as the world's reserve currency, replacing the US dollar. There is a long way to go before such an event could occur—but the possibility is interesting to entertain.

- Much of the crypto landscape feels like the 'Wild West' right now, so it's important to exercise caution when investing in 'opportunities.' Some will be highly successful and make enormous returns for early investors, while others will fail and disappear without a trace.

With just this basic understanding, you will now be naturally 'alert' to news and developments in the crypto space. The pace of development is like nothing we've seen before. The speed is blistering and outstrips the pace of the development of internet technology. It would be a brave person to forecast the impact of crypto on us in the coming years. But I think it's safe to assume that we will grossly underestimate what this new class of technology will achieve. Just like we did for the Internet.

I hope that the concluding section of this book feels like a beginning for you. In the introduction, I encouraged you to 'play' in the crypto sand pit so that you learn through active participation. So now's the time to ask yourself if you think the demand for bitcoin will be higher in 5-10 years. If your answer is yes, then it's time to stick your toe in the market. If your answer is no, then sit on the sidelines.

A SHORT MESSAGE FROM THE AUTHOR

Did you enjoy the book? I really hope so. And I hope that you're also now the proud owner of some bitcoin!

If you enjoyed *"What is this bitcoin thing?"* I'd be super grateful to hear your thoughts on the review area of Amazon. Feedback helps me to improve my writing and create the best books I can. Even a short 1-2 sentence review would mean the world.

Many readers don't know how hard reviews are to come by and how much they help an author—especially a first-time author!

I would be incredibly grateful if you could just take 60 seconds to write a brief review on Amazon—even if it's just a few sentences!

Thank you for taking the time to share your thoughts.

And finally, please don't forget to download your free copy of the *Crypto Survival Quick Start Guide*.

This is an essential companion as you start your exploration of the crypto world. It will keep you safe. It's an action summary and checklist that will show you:

- **How to DYOR—"Do Your Own Research"**
- **Dangers of crypto to avoid—and how to stay SAFE**
- **Specific NEXT STEPS to further your learning**

I've created the guide to be fun, fast to consume, and action-oriented. It's precisely what I wish I'd had five years ago when I first dipped my toes into crypto waters.

Get your Crypto Survival Quick Start Guide here: https://marcohodd.com/crypto-survival

ACKNOWLEDGEMENTS

This is the first book I've ever written. I haven't written more than a page or two at a time since I left full-time education—so I hope I've done an OK job! It's possibly one of the hardest things I've ever done.

Places, rather than people, have helped me write. The loud silence of McGregor's Farm in Glynde shaped the plan and the early ideas. Then, regular changes in location kept me 'in the zone' to complete the book—Marko's Mediterranean apartment in Split, Brown Coffee's massive cool concrete rooms in Siem Reap, and Shibui Concept, a vinyl-playing coffee shop hidden away somewhere in Saigon.

In the coming weeks, I will gladly receive the enthusiasm and encouragement of friends and family to begin the (somewhat daunting) task of beginning the second volume—*"What is this crypto thing?"*

Printed in Great Britain
by Amazon